CONCILIUM

Religion in the Eighties

CONCILIUM

Editorial Directors

Concilium 138 (8/1980): Ecumenism

CONFLICTING WAYS OF INTERPRETING THE BIBLE

Edited by

Hans Küng

and

Jürgen Moltmann

English Language Editor
Marcus Lefébure

T. & T. CLARK LTD.
Edinburgh

THE SEABURY PRESS
New York

October 1980
T. & T. Clark Ltd., 36 George Street, Edinburgh EH2 2LQ
ISBN: 0 567 30018 8

The Seabury Press, 815 Second Avenue, New York, N.Y. 10017
ISBN: 0 8164 2280 X

Library of Congress Catalog Card No.: 80 50582

Printed in Scotland by William Blackwood & Sons Ltd., Edinburgh

Concilium: Monthly except July and August.
Subscriptions 1980: All countries (except U.S.A. and Canada) £23·00 postage and handling included; U.S.A. and Canada $54.00 postage and handling included. (Second class postage licence 541-530 at New York, N.Y.) Subscription distribution in U.S. by Expeditors of the Printed Word Ltd., 527 Madison Avenue, Suite 1217, New York, N.Y. 10022.

CONTENTS

Editorial
JÜRGEN MOLTMANN and HANS KÜNG   vii

Part I
Scientific Exegesis Today

Is Historical Criticism out of date?
CHRISTIAN HARTLICH   3

Two Types of Exegesis with a Linguistic Basis
RENÉ KIEFFER   9

Why a Materialist Reading?
FERNANDO BELO   17

Is a Psycho-Analytical Reading of the Bible Possible?
DOMINIQUE STEIN   24

Part II
Practical Exegesis Today

A Jewish Exegesis of the Walking on the Water
PINCHAS LAPIDE   35

How the Bible is Interpreted in some Basic Christian Communities in Brazil
CARLOS MESTERS   41

The Black Church and the Future in South Africa
ALLAN BOESAK   47

Feminist Perspectives on New Testament Exegesis
BERNADETTE BROOTEN   55

Part III

The Authority of the Church in the Interpretation of Scripture
   JOSEF BLANK   65

The Fundamentalist Understanding of Scripture
   JAMES BARR   70

The Biblical Basis for the Dogmatic Way of Speaking
   ALEXANDRE GANOCZY   75

Documentation

A Letter on Christology and Infallibility
   HANS KÜNG   85

Contributors   98

Editorial

THE Church of Christ has for many historical reasons split into a multiplicity of Churches, confessions and denominations. All Christian Churches, denominations and confessions do, however, have one thing in common: the Bible. As long as the sacred Scripture is opened, read and proclaimed in all Christian Churches, knowledge about Christ's community cannot perish. The quest for the ecumenical unity of Christ's Church goes on as long as the authority of the Bible is acknowledged. As often as we keep returning to Scripture we also keep seeking to turn towards the common ecumenical future of the divided Church. This is why Scripture and the common interpretation of Scripture are the principal instruments of the ecumenical movement.

The trouble is that the authority of Scripture and its proper meaningful interpretation are themselves disputed nowadays in most churches. The 'conflict about the Bible' cuts right across most churches. New boundaries are forming. New insights are emerging. Many Christians are learning to read the Bible with new eyes as a result of the company they keep with other men. Our point is that the conflict about different ways of interpreting the Bible should not be judged only in a negative way. No effort is too great where truth is at stake, and the passion of the struggle is a measure of the truth involved. There are many exegetical methods which complement each other. They display the full richness of the biblical testimony to the truth. There are, however, also methods which contradict each other, as, for instance the historico-critical and the fundamentalist methods do. Such differences compel us to think for ourselves and to make our own decisions. In this issue we have represented both mutually complementary and mutually contradictory interpretations.

We have organised this issue in such a way that the contributions about *scientific exegesis today* appear first. We wanted to exhibit the new forms of materialist, linguistic and psycho-analytic interpretations. One of the basic questions left in the cultural wake of the European Enlightenment remains, however, the historico-critical understanding of the truth of sayings handed down to us. Many people very understandably still find it a stone of stumbling, nor are the devout themselves exempt.

The interpretation of the Bible is not merely the object of scientific methods but the banner of given communities. So, under the rather unsatisfactory title of *Practical Exegesis Today*, we have investigated Jewish exegesis, Black and feminist interpretations and the new familiarity with the Bible developed by the Basic Communities of Latin America. And certain confessionally controversial questions about the interpretation and use of Scripture are discussed in Part III.

We wanted to avoid getting drawn into too abstract methodological discussions and so we took the liberty of asking the authors, so far as possible, to display the method they were discussing by reference to the interpretation of the story of Jesus's walking on the water described in Mark 6:45-52. This concreteness makes the complementarity and the conflicts of the various interpretations adduced perspicuous and exciting. They should serve to draw the reader into dialogue with the Bible. Dialogue with the Bible, dialogue with each other about the Bible, and dialogue with him to the truth of whom the Bible testifies are for us the heart of ecumenism.

Translated by John Maxwell

JÜRGEN MOLTMANN
HANS KÜNG

PART I

Scientific Exegesis Today

Christian Hartlich

Is Historical Criticism out of date?

OF FUNDAMENTAL significance for Christian theology is the question whether or to what extent the method of historical criticism is applicable to the interpretation of the Bible and of the sacred history recounted in it. Depending on the answer given to this question are three different directions theology can follow: (*a*) a dogmatic one that rejects any criticism of the miraculous events recounted in the Bible as the offspring of mankind's wanton insolence; (*b*) one concerned to reconcile the dogmatic approach with historical criticism and one which, without any profound consideration of hermeneutical principles, interprets the New Testament stories of miracles as legends but nevertheless clings with all its might to the resurrection of Jesus as a historical fact, albeit of a singular nature; and (*c*) a third tendency that applies historical criticism thoroughly and consistently and labels the Bible's 'sacred history' as mythological, including the supernatural aspects of the story of Jesus. This last tendency meets with the strongest resistance on the part of the institutionalised Churches, whose dearest wish is that the method of historical criticism would be proved to be out of date so that, on the basis of this proof, they could return to a theological situation such as existed before the emergence of this method.

As a matter of fact the Bible stories were read for centuries without any attempt being made to apply any kind of historical criticism to the events that were recounted. Right up to the time of the Reformation sacred Scripture was regarded as the inerrant witness of divine revelation. Even when it comes to Luther's understanding of the Bible, considerations based on historical criticism do not yet have any kind of significance, as can be seen from three examples. When Luther was once asked at dinner what view should be taken of the three days' sojourn spent by the prophet Jonah in the belly of a great fish, he answered that he would regard this story as a deceitful fable and refuse to believe it were it not for the fact that it was in sacred Scripture (*neque crederem, nisi in sacris libris esset scripta*). The same reason placed beyond doubt as far as he was concerned the reality of the miracle reported in the book of Joshua, when the sun and moon were stayed in their course until Joshua had taken vengeance on the people of his enemies. The medieval context that framed Luther's ideas of chronology is shown by his *Supputatio annorum mundi* of 1540: on the basis of indications in the Bible he calculated the date for the creation of the world as 3960 B.C.

1. THE DILEMMA OF DOGMATIC THEOLOGY IN THE FACE OF THE EMERGENCE OF HISTORICAL CRITICISM

It was barely a century later that historical criticism, which up till then had confined itself to secular history and the legendary traditions of the middle ages, turned its attention to the Bible. Thus the outstanding exegete and orientalist Johannes Drusius (1550-1616) remarked on chapter 4 of Exodus that on secular and ephemeral matters the prophets sometimes indulged in fantastic ideas. To attacks from theologians who took issue with his style of exegesis free from dogmatic prejudices, his answer was: 'I am not a theologian. "What are you then?" you will ask. I am a Christian, a friend of truth.' (*Non sum theologus. Quid igitur es? inquies. Christianus sum, philalethes sum.*)

The point of this statement lies in the way it presents being a Christian and being truthful as an inseparable unity in contrast to the life of the dogmatic theologian, who thinks that for the sake of his presumed orthodoxy he is obliged to obstruct the findings of historical criticism.

A little later, in 1618, Abraham Schultetus aroused considerable attention by discussing the question whether a theologian was allowed to call on non-theological disciplines or profane authors in the interpretation of scripture. His answer was a decisive yes, which implicitly carried with it the view that the historical reports to be found in scripture cannot lay claim to rules of interpretation other than those applying to the writings of profane authors.

In these relatively early statements the difficulties are already beginning to appear that theology sees as increasingly entangling it through the development of historical criticism. These problems were impressed on the general consciousness by two works that have to be regarded as epoch-making for the spread of historical criticism.

1677 saw the publication in Paris of the *Histoire critique du Vieux Testament* by the Oratorian Richard Simon. The fifth chapter was headed: 'Moses cannot be the author of all the books attributed to him.' This thesis, which in any case Spinoza had already put forward, was fatal for the author and his work. At Bossuet's instigation Simon was expelled from the Oratory and the Paris edition destroyed. It took over 250 years before the Pontifical Biblical Commission declared in its letter to Cardinal Suhard. Archbishop of Paris, that today there was no longer anyone who 'does not admit a progressive accretion to the Mosaic laws due to the social and religious conditions of subsequent ages, a progression which is also shown in the historical accounts' (DS 3863)—a statement which only two years later was given a restrictive commentary in the encyclical *Humani generis* of 1950 (DS 3898-9).

A short time after the *Histoire critique du Vieux Testament* there appeared (1695-7) the *Dictionnaire historique et critique* by the Protestant Pierre Bayle. The principle *de omnibus dubitandum* was applied to matters of history. It was only through methodically doubting everything reported to us in the way of events in documents of the past that historical truth could be found out.

Thanks to Simon and Bayle the term 'critical history' or the epithet 'historico-critical' came to provide an indication in the title of numerous theological publications that collectively were concerned to answer the question whether and to what extent historical truth could be drawn from the stories to be found in the Bible.

It had become necessary to add the epithet 'critical' to the term 'history' since *historia* could mean any kind of report about what had occurred in the past without reference to whether what was involved was a *historia fabulosa* or a *historia vera*. Even today in colloquial French the expression *C'est une histoire* means something like: 'Pull the other one, that's a likely tale.' And if one looks up the word 'story' in an English or American dictionary one will find some such definition as 'a narrative or recital of an event, or a series of events, *whether real or fictitious*'.

Historical criticism exposes this ambiguity to be found in the use of the terms *historia*, *histoire*, *Geschichte*, an ambiguity avoided in English by the distinction between 'history' and 'story'. The addition of the epithet 'critical' reveals the aim of distinguishing between accounts of events that are imaginary and fictitious and those that are real and verifiable. After a long process of trial and error this aim was realised in a method which we shall now see applied to the story of Jesus walking on the water.

2. THE STORY OF JESUS WALKING ON THE LAKE OF GENNESARET FROM THE POINT OF VIEW OF HISTORICAL CRITICISM

The fundamental and primary task of critical historical scholarship is to establish whether the events recounted in reports of the past actually took place and whether they took place in the way that they have been recounted to us. Such an investigation is unavoidable because in the case of no human being does his or her individual subjective opinion that an event has actually taken place guarantee the objective nature of this opinion. Even eye-witnesses and others as close as possible to the events they are reporting can make mistakes.

This applies to the Bible too. The criticial historian is not therefore content with an exegesis which remains within the conceptual context of the biblical authors and restricts itself simply to reproducing the literal sense of the text. Instead he or she goes beyond what the author intended in order to examine the truth of his accounts of events, and the criterion for deciding how truthful these accounts are depends on the outcome of the critical process.

(a) The findings of exegesis

Jesus walking on the lake of Gennesaret is recounted in three places in the gospels: Mark 6:45-52; Matt. 14:22-33; and John 6:16-22.

While these accounts show considerable differences in detail, they agree in their presentation of the miraculous event. After the miraculous feeding of the five thousand Jesus withdrew to be alone. His disciples meanwhile set out across the lake in a boat. Night had already fallen when a strong wind blew up and put them in danger. Jesus came walking over the water. The disciples were frightened at this sight and were unsure whether it was a ghost or really him. Jesus made himself known to them with the words: 'Take heart, it is I; have no fear.' Through Jesus's arrival the occupants of the boat remain preserved from all harm.

No cause for doubt is raised by the fact of a boat getting into difficulties on the lake of Gennesaret in stormy weather at night. But that a man should defy the law of gravity and walk on water as on dry land goes against all our experience.

The point is, of course, continually being made throughout the gospels that Jesus is not a human being in the ordinary sense of the word but is at the same time the Son of God. The accounts of miracles accomplished by Jesus confirm the truth of this assertion: given someone who is able to calm a raging storm through his word of command, who can walk on the water, who raises the dead to life and himself overcomes death through his resurrection, what else can he be other than the Son of God?

This rationale behind the accounts of miracles also governs the three versions of the story of Jesus walking on the water. Different accounts may be given of the effect of this miracle on those who observed it, but ultimately the conclusion that the story-teller wishes his audience to draw from it is one and the same: Jesus is the Son of God.

In Mark the disciples are quite beside themselves with astonishment at Jesus's appearance and the associated calming of the storm. They are as little able to comprehend this fresh demonstration of his miraculous powers as they were able to comprehend the miracle of the feeding of the five thousand as a sign of Jesus's role as the Messiah. The fact that they are so upset is an indirect testimony to the magnitude of the miracle.

The theme of a miracle providing accreditation of Jesus's status and role is also to be found in the Johannine version. The people's question: 'When did you come here?' (John 6:25) can to the evangelist's mind be answered only by the fact that the Son of God is not subject to the limitations that apply to all human beings in moving from one place to another.

Matthew's account is the most detailed thanks to the introduction of the episode involving Peter. After Jesus had approached the boat and made himself known to the disciples by saying: 'It is I,' Peter said to him: 'Lord, if it is you, bid me come to you on the water'—in other words, do something to confirm for me that you are who you claim to be. Jesus meets this demand by saying: 'Come.'

The disciples, convinced by these proofs of Jesus's miraculous powers, fall down and worship him and acclaim him with one voice: 'Truly you are the Son of God.'

Thus on the one hand the miracle of Jesus walking on the water confirms and ratifies his divine powers; on the other hand Jesus's powers confirm and ratify the miracle. He who is able to walk on water is the Son of God; he who is the Son of God is able to walk on water. Both assertions are equally unverifiable and each confirms and ratifies the other—just like a house of cards composed of one card leaning against another with none being able to stand up on its own.

(b) The procedure of historical criticism

In its three different versions the story of Jesus walking on the water thus recounts a miraculous manifestation of his being the Son of God.

Historical criticism recognises that, from the point of view of discerning what actually happened in the past, these stories are valueless. What is involved is a story intended as true but the truth of which can in no case be established by those telling it. A man walking on the water goes against all known laws of experience. Beyond this, the factual reality of a divine or supernatural cause at work on the part of the Son of God is something that obviously cannot be proved or demonstrated. The objective reality of events can only be established as long as they are in agreement with the general conditions that govern our perception of what is really real, as opposed to what is merely presumed to be real, and as long as they can be accommodated within the context of experience that up to now has been confirmed as not admitting any exceptions.

Statements about miraculous and supernatural events, and above all statements about an immediate involvement or manifestation on the part of God or his Son as well as of other supernatural beings, are unverifiable in principle. This means that in no case can we distinguish whether the events and data described in such statements as real have a merely subjective existence in the opinion, imagination and contention of the person making them or whether they enjoy an external objective reality independent of this. To put it another way: if we bring such statements within the framework we use for perceiving external reality, it is in principle impossible to distinguish among them between true statements and false ones, and maintaining their truth is equally impossible. If in fact one wanted justifiably to maintain the truth of such statements, one would have to be able to offer criteria according to which it could be discerned with universal validity that there was an external objective reality that corresponded to the external supernatural reality or involvement put forward in these statements. What would thus need to be provided for statements of this kind, in a manner that corresponded to the particular nature of their objectivity, would be the equivalent of what the empirical method is able to supply in the case of statements about the empirical objectivity of what can be perceived through the senses: that is, to provide a methodical and universally valid foundation for proceeding from the conception of reality to the reality of what is conceived. But in the case of supernatural reality and efficacity this kind of empirical method does not exist, and this is the reason why historical criticism treats all statements which as far as their form is concerned are talking about the reality of events of this kind as statements whose objectivity it is fundamentally impossible to demonstrate.

(c) Sacred history as a historical and as a theological problem

On the basis of its classification of miraculous events as events that did not really occur historical criticism goes on to ask what conditions must have existed in the subjective consciousness of the persons recounting sacred history so that they recount miraculous events as if they had really taken place even though they had not actually taken place. How can we explain that in telling their stories the biblical writers seem hardly to be worried, if worried at all, by the question that today affects everyone who attempts to provide a truthful and responsible account of what has happened, the question whether these events actually took place?

The answer to this question is given by showing that the phenomenon of sacred history arises only in epochs and societies in which there has not yet taken place any thorough-going critical reflection on the conditions needed for statements about past events claiming to be true. Corresponding to this is the observation that the recounting of sacred miraculous history largely disappears when two things become predominant in a society: awareness of the necessity of verification, and recognition of the criteria that are needed for this. In the absence of such reflection those who recount sacred history allow heterogeneous elements to mingle with each other in their narratives, elements between which modern criticism is forced to make fundamental distinctions from the point of view of establishing the facts. Their method of thinking and narrating can be labelled naïve to the extent that in their stories they mix what is unreal and miraculous with what is historical and can be established.

This change in perception is an epochal event and strikes at the root of the traditional understanding of Christianity. When we hear a story the first question has always been whether, according to the criteria for recognising reality, it really happened or not. With regard to the miraculous stories recounted in the Bible, as with regard to the corresponding stories connected with other religions, we cannot avoid the answer that these statements may look like history as far as their form is concerned but do not offer any verifiable, real history.

For the accounts of miracles in the New Testament this means that the evangelists use the form of history in order to summon their audience to belief through the indirect appeal of this manner of narration. Exegetically it can be shown that in themselves the stories about Jesus which were handed on and which circulated in the original Christian community about the manifestation of the Son of God represented material that could be moulded and shaped according to the particular literary intention of the person handling it, an intention that in any case was not determined by the concept of objective factual reality. In other words, statements by the evangelists apparently describing objective events have a variable function at the service of a fundamental intention which is not directed at the audience recognising and accepting factual data in keeping with the principles of historical criticism, but is calling on the audience to grasp the possibility of new life.

Anyone, therefore, who treats the apparently historical statements of the miracle-stories in the gospels as assertions of fact is taking them out of the functional context that exegesis shows them to have and exposes them to the rigour of the modern concept of objective fact, something that is the product of the scientific outlook of the post-medieval world. This misinterpretation surrenders these statements to a process of criticism from which they are bound to emerge the losers.

One consequence of this mistaken hermeneutical attitude is the disastrous theological error of taking the sacred history recounted in the gospels, ignoring its expressive role, and turning it into the primary object of faith. A Church or theology which, in an age that no longer thinks in mythical terms, asks people to regard mythical statements as historical statements and as true in that sense, and which proclaims the fulfilment of this demand as the fundamental act of faith, reduces Christianity to the level of mythodoxy. Belief in God's forgiveness is something essentially other than regarding as historically true what can be perceived to be a pseudo-historical account of God's forgiveness.

The method of historical criticism is not outmoded. All it does, in a manner that is representative of mankind's concern for the truth, is to apply methodically to statements about past events the conditions and criteria for perceiving reality that man has at his disposal.

So far theology has avoided coming to grips with historical criticism by accusing it of adopting arbitrary presuppositions that are therefore in need of revision. Once it is recognised that the method of historical criticism has its roots in the structure of human perception and epistemology, then only a theology that allies itself to historical criticism will be able to have an ecumenical future.

Translated by Robert Nowell

René Kieffer

Two Types of Exegesis with a Linguistic Basis

1. LINGUISTICS AND BIBLICAL SCIENCES

'DEPENDING on one's viewpoint, linguistics came into being either during the fifth century B.C., or in 1816 with Bopp, or in 1916 with de Saussure, or in 1926 with Troubetzkoy, or in 1956 with Chomsky.'[1] These words from a somewhat prudent specialist in linguistics encourage us to retain a sense of perspective. Biblical exegesis has always been in close contact with various branches of philology. Linking this great tradition to linguistics is simply a matter of definition.

When, in France, C. Lévi-Strauss, R. Barthes, M. Foucault or J. Lacan—working in a completely different field from that of exegesis—claim to have been inspired by work done in linguistics, there is no doubt that they are taking F. de Saussure as its originator, even if, on occasion, these brilliant authors treat linguistic concepts somewhat disrespectfully.

De Saussure's basic tenets are well known: the formal system of language (*langue*) is placed in opposition to the spoken word (*parole*), the diachronic to the synchronic; the significant is distinguished from the referent, and syntagmatic relationships from associative ones (which Hjelmslev calls 'para-digmatic'). The point of departure is clear: in contrast to F. Bopp's system of comparative linguistics, which traces the historical evolution of languages, de Saussure wants to consider them in their synchronic state, as systems in which it is the relationships between words which are of crucial importance.[2] Along these lines, Troubetzkoy's phonology will provide a model of linguistic study, by its method of detailing the 'distinguishing' features of language: 'Phonology must only provide for sounds which fulfil a definite function within a language.'[3] Study along these same lines will extend into the field of syntax, to come to a halt with N. Chomsky's system which, in theory, generates by various processes of transformation the possible utterances of a given language.

Still in this vein, it remains for us to consider the semantic aspect. In France, C. Bremond, T. Todorov, and also A. J. Greimas and his school have devoted themselves particularly to this area of study. In Germany, we find a school of 'Textlinguistik', like that of G. Weinold,[4] which is attuned to the phenomena of human communication, and which, as a result, develops not only a semantic but also a pragmatic study of texts. In the United States, 'discourse analysis' with varying grammatical starting-points, passes from non-semantic formalism, as with Z. S. Harris, to an integrative study of semantics in the case of, for example, E. A. Nida (who is particularly concerned with the problems of biblical translation). But nowadays such national barriers scarcely continue to exist: different forms of linguistics are readily transmitted from country to country.[5]

It is clear that biblical exegesis can profit on several counts from the linguistic researches which have been summarily evinced here. As regards vocabulary, a study of semantic fields may cause us to look again at the various Greek or Hebrew words at present listed separately, in alphabetical order, in the dictionaries we normally use. In this respect, J. Barr has justifiably criticised our habitual tool, the *Theologisches Wörterbuch* of G. Kittel and G. Friedrich.[6] As regards grammar, we can expect a fresh presentation of Greek and Hebrew syntax along the lines taken by Chomsky. Our theological synthesis of the New and Old Testaments will, increasingly, have to take into account the different 'corpora' which have been analysed, as well as having to distinguish more satisfactorily the synchronic and diachronic points of view regarding the presentation of material.[7]

But, above all, it is with regard to exegesis and commentary that linguistic studies, especially those which treat the semantic aspect of language, can cause us to reconsider. Within the narrow limits of this article, I should like to apply two patterns of linguistic analysis to Mark 6:45-52 and its parallels, in order to illustrate the potential of these new approaches.

2. A LINGUISTIC ANALYSIS OF MARK 6:45-52 AND PARALLELS ON THE PATTERN OFFERED BY NIDA, TABER AND OLSSON

Nida's 'nuclear structures'[8] are based on an analysis of the sentence which considers the verb as a kind of centre around which the other traditional elements of the sentence (subject, object, adverb etc.) are grouped like 'satellites'. Thus, a text may be rewritten in the form of elementary sentences ('kernel sentences') which present each minimal item of information offered in the text. 'Information units' will be an equally good name for these sentences (in a narrative text, Olsson calls them 'event units'). In our example (Mark 6:45-52), the structure of events may be rewritten in the form of about 24 units, of which one (v. 50b) constitutes a unit of dialogue (or rather of monologue, since only Jesus is speaking in this case; in Matthew, this unit is developed into a true dialogue with Peter and the disciples). Let us simply list the first event units in Mark's text: (i) Jesus makes his disciples get back into the boat. (ii) Jesus wants them to go ahead of him to the other side. (iii) Jesus sends the crowd away himself. (iv) Jesus goes up to the mountains to pray. (v) Evening comes. (vi) The boat is in the middle of the sea. (vii) Jesus is alone on the land, etc. Each unit may be studied as a self-contained entity and in its relationships to other units. This rewriting of the text enables us to perceive more clearly each new element that appears. It also facilitates the task of isolating the *eight constraining factors* which, according to Nida and Taber, are a feature of the structure of any text. These 'constraints' are called 'universals of discourse'.

(a) *Terminal features and points of transition*

The first two factors concern the text as a whole: the beginning and end points (which we may call, with Olsson, the 'terminal features') and the points of transition. In our text, those at the beginning create a situation of estrangement between Jesus and the disciples which is responsible for generating the account which follows. Jesus himself takes the initiative (at least in Mark and Matthew, but not in John). The final point in Mark's account emphasises the link with the preceding miracle of the loaves and the disciples' lack of understanding (see a similar case of incomprehension in Mark 8:17 after the second miracle of the loaves). In Matthew's version (14:22-33), Mark's final feature has been changed: there is no link with the miracle of the loaves. Instead of incomprehension, there is a scene of adoration with an explicit acknowledgement: 'Truly, you are the Son of God!'). As the terminal features are crucial to the understanding of the text as a whole, it is clear that the miracle of Jesus walking on the water and stilling the wind has a different function in Matthew: from a scene of lack of recognition, it is turned into a scene of acknowledgement. In John's account (6:16-21) the terminal feature leaves out the sudden lull: the disciples want to take Jesus on board. Mysteriously, the boat immediately arrives at the shore they were bound for. The attainment of a goal, with Jesus's help, is here the final feature of the account.

The transitional features in Mark's text are well known: the accumulation of 'and' and 'immediately', repetition (v. 45: 'he dismissed the crowd'; v. 46: 'having taken leave of them';[9] see also the use of the verb 'see' in vv. 49-50). It is not necessary to assume, as does M.-E. Boismard,[10] the existence of two sources of documentation to explain this 'duality', which is frequent in Mark. Matthew removes those repetitions which he considers redundant.

(b) *Chronological, spatial and logical features*

Following on from those factors which are relevant to the whole text, let us look more closely at the three factors which determine the events in the account: chronological features, spatial features and logical features.

(i) There is a chronological problem: why is the boat already in the middle of the sea in the evening (hence at about the first watch of the night), when Jesus does not come until the end of the fourth watch, that is between three o'clock and six o'clock in the morning? 'Cultural' connotations may partially explain this distension: the 'evening' is held to be the onset of the threat of darkness (see earlier in Mark 4:35, which leads into the scene where the storm is calmed); on the other hand, 'morning' is the time when God grants his help (see, for example, Exod. 14:24 and Ps. 119:147, but also Mark 16:2). With the coming of Jesus, night yields to day.

(ii) Spatial features are particularly important in our text: the disciples are supposed to go ahead of Jesus to the other side, towards Bethsaida, but in fact, after the lull, they arrive at Gennesaret (Mark 6:53). The topography thus stresses a reorientation (as a result of Jesus's intervention?). Jesus leaves to go into the mountains, a symbolic place, where one can talk to God. The boat is in the middle of the sea,[11] which could represent the centre around which the natural elements are unleashed. Jesus is alone on the land, a stable element, far from the disciples (this last point is emphasised by Matthew). The fact that he walks on the sea, as one would on land, prolongs this element of stability. Jesus comes towards the disciples, which signifies a move to help. But he seems to be passing them by (only in Mark's account): this may be understood in the light of the 'cultural' code as signifying the passage of divine glory (see Exod. 33:19, 22; 34:6; 1 Kings 19:11). Jesus's walk is described 'objectively', and not from the disciples' point of view, which accounts for their surprise and confusion. Jesus's arrival on board the boat occasions the sudden lull: he is thus presented as an element of stability in the face of the unleashed forces of nature.

(iii) The logic of the text requires the situation of estrangement at the beginning in order to give full significance to the union between Jesus and the confused disciples.[12] The description of the walk on the water as a kind of divine manifestation (see Job 9:8; Pss. 65:8; 77:17; 89:10; 107:29) and the fact that the disciples are not prepared for this are responsible for a misinterpretation: they think they are seeing a ghost, perhaps a dead man returned to life. The lull does not come about whilst Jesus is walking on the water, but when he gets into the boat. This indicates that we need to distinguish two stages: the walk on water as a scene of manifestation and recognition, followed by Jesus boarding the boat as one of rescue (see Mark 4:35-41). Some exegetical scholars, like E. Lohmeyer,[13] have, as a result of this double logic in the text, tried to see in it a coalescence of two originally separate accounts. Yet our text points precisely to the unity between the misinterpreted divine manifestation and the rescue.

(c) The characters and the basic description of the scene

Now let us consider two further factors, the first of which is concerned with the characters which figure in our text and the second with the general setting for the episode.

(i) It is clear that Jesus always takes the initiative, especially in Mark: he creates the situation of estrangement at the outset (in Mark and Matthew, not in John), just as he 'sees' (emphasised by Mark only) from a distance the plight of the disciples and comes to their aid. The disciples are portrayed in the light of their reactions to the divine manifestation. They misunderstand when they think they see a ghost, and they are no wiser than before, during the miracle of the loaves; their hearts are hardened. The darkness, the wind and the sea are hostile elements from the disciples' point of view, although subject to the power of Jesus.

(ii) If we look at the features which set the scene for the participants and the events (Nida and Taber call them 'foregrounding' and 'backgrounding'), we notice a strong contrast between Jesus praying alone in the mountains and the disciples struggling amidst the difficulties at sea. These two contrasted scenes increase the stature of Jesus to the detriment of that of the disciples. The reader is prepared for the sight of Jesus completely in control of the unleashed elements: his walking on the water and calming the storm result from his special contact with God in the mountains.

(d) The standpoint of the author

It remains for us to consider the eighth feature, which concerns the standpoint of the author. This is located after Christ's resurrection, amidst the specific problems of a congregation encouraged to believe in the risen Lord. In Luke (24:37ff.), Christ appears to his disciples and points out to them that a 'spirit' does not have substance as he does. In the scene from Mark we are analysing here, we are concerned, in theory, with Jesus before the resurrection. But, at the same time, we cannot disregard the post-Paschal situation, where Jesus must not simply be presented as a 'ghost' who has come back to life. He is the one who can say: "It is I", and thus demonstrate his power over the cosmos. The disciples fail to grasp Jesus's identity, just as they do not understand the divine manifestation in the miracle of the loaves. Jesus is the Lord, who, even before his resurrection, gives proof of his privileged relationship with God.

Nida and Taber confine themselves to describing the eight features which are characteristic of any discourse. However, a hermeneutic study of the text forces us to look beyond these specific observations and consider, with B. Olsson, the full import of the text. In Mark, it is a case not only of the account of a saving manifestation (*rettende Epiphaniegeschichte*)—this is stressed, for example, by W. Pesch, in line with G. Theissen[14]—nor, as R. Otto thought, of a 'charismatic apparition', but essentially a case of misapprehension of the saving manifestation. This misapprehension must be set against all the other indications in Mark's gospel of the recognition of Christ's identity. The Messianic secret is an important element of this recognition.

In Matthew, on the other hand, the scene is transformed into an acknowledgement of increasing faith in Christ. At the start there is the beginning of a response from Peter, who dares to set out on the water, but who sinks when his faith fails him. At the end, all the disciples acknowledge their explicit recognition: 'Truly, you are the Son of God!'.

In John, there is less emphasis on saving and recognition in favour of the divine manifestation: 'It is I!'.

The method of Nida, Taber and Olsson thus allows us to integrate some of the elements of traditional exegesis, such as the associative relationships of the expressions 'evening', 'morning', 'sea', 'he meant to pass them by', 'the mountains', etc. Such a reading can lead towards a consideration of the pragmatic aspects: what could be and what should be the response of anyone reading this text who is aware of the difficult problem of apprehending Jesus's ultimate identity?

3. A LINGUISTIC ANALYSIS OF MARK 6:45-52 AND PARALLELS USING GREIMAS'S METHOD

The type of exegesis based on the linguistic pattern offered by Nida, Taber and Olsson does not really deal adequately with one important element in our account: the 'narrative' aspect itself. With this in mind, we will look at Greimas's method[15] which was first developed in connection with the formalisation of Russian folk tales by V. Propp. The pattern of the method is as follows:

(i) First, our attention is drawn to the 'active' components of the text and the different 'functions' of the passage as a narrative account.

(ii) This study of the network of processes and relationships which serve to generate the 'narrative organisation' of the text is then completed by an analysis of the 'discursive component', which deals with the 'network of imagery' and the 'thematic roles' in the text. The narrative and discursive components are part of the surface structure of the text.

(iii) Thirdly, to attain the deep structure of the text, linguists of Greimas's school use the 'semiotic square', which makes it possible to determine the 'essential structure of the meaning'.

(a) The narrative programmes

Rewritten in Greimas's 'semiotic' language, Mark's text presents us with different narrative programmes. First, there is that of Jesus, who sends his disciples ahead of him to the other side and who, having dismissed the crowd, goes to pray alone in the mountains. Following on from this, the programme of the disciples is to arrive at the other side before him, but 'adversities', the darkness, the wind which is against them, and the rough sea prevent them from realising their programme. Thus, the disciples are cut off from the aim they are pursuing: to arrive on the other side before Jesus. The narrative as such requires an 'operative subject', a 'hero', who by virtue of his 'abilities' can transform the wretched situation of the disciples. Jesus has these abilities: he 'sees' from a distance his disciples in difficulty. Normally, this knowledge should make him 'want' to help them, but Mark's text also indicates that he wants to pass them by. This ambiguity emphasises, as in the scene of the loaves, that Jesus's 'will' is not merely limited to making good a lack. The 'power' of Jesus is conveyed by the walk on the water and the sudden lull. Jesus's ability as regards 'knowledge', 'will' and 'power' is therefore partly brought into play in a struggle or 'performance' which is successful: the sea becomes calm. But the 'glorification' of the 'hero' is incomplete: the disciples fail to recognise their Master, who is obliged to take the initiative of revealing himself to them. In the same way, the end of the account emphasises that the disciples have understood no more than with the miracle of the loaves. The passage which follows our text, with the healings at Gennesaret, gives, in this sense, more evidence of success: 'the people recognised Jesus' (v. 54), but, in the eyes of the author, even this recognition is probably ambiguous. The fact that the disciples have not understood is linked to an 'inability to know': their hearts are hardened. Their powers of interpretation are distinguished by astonishment and not by faith (in contrast to what happens in Matthew's account, with Peter's deepening faith and, above all, the disciples' public acknowledgement).

(b) The thematic roles

The link which the author himself establishes with the scene of the loaves invites us to consider the 'thematic roles' of Mark 6:30-53 taken as a whole. In Mark 6:32f. we find that travelling on foot is set in opposition to travelling by boat. In 6:45-53, the paradox is that those who travel by boat (the normal thing on water) are unable to continue their journey, whilst Jesus himself uses walking as a means of setting out on the water. The sky, which figures in 6:41, before the miracle of the loaves, is also evoked here when Jesus prays in the mountains. Thus we can establish the 'network of imagery', where the land, sea and sky are set in relation to one another.[16]

(c) The network of imagery

In a 'semiotic square', it is possible for us to convey the discursive component of this episode in terms of the conjunction of land and sea, as opposed to their normal disjunction:[17] Jesus walks on the sea as one walks on land, which is not 'normal'. In so doing, he fulfils in his person the conjunction between land (with its component of stability) and sea, thanks to his special relationship with heaven (the prayer in the mountains).

As regards the 'network of imagery', one can also discern two axes: that of sentience and that of faith. The disciples, lacking faith, are not able to perceive Jesus's relationship to the natural elements. That is because they are, on the axis of sentience, stupefied, and believe they are seeing a ghost. Jesus encourages them, on the sentient level, not to be afraid. But what they must do and what they do not manage to do, is to turn, on the axis of faith, from hardness of heart to that openness of heart which will enable them to recognise the cosmic dimensions of Jesus, in whom heaven, earth and sea come together in harmony.

4. SOME CONCLUSIONS

We have only been able to use these two types of exegesis based on linguistic examples in a very summary way. Other methods could be advanced.[18] Greimas's semiotics systematise those narrative and discursive elements which the method of Nida, Taber and Olsson leaves more in the open. Consequently, it is easier to introduce traditional philological approaches to the grammatical meaning, the style and cultural background of the text into this latter method. Greimas's pattern has the advantage of giving more serious consideration to the narrative aspect of our text. For an account like this is not merely a juxtaposition of different themes or events, but a coherent whole which follows a specific 'programme'.

The analyses suggested here can, in the context of a different linguistic approach, like that of G. Weinold, be extended more explicitly into the realms of 'pragmatism': what does this text mean to those who read Mark? The very lack of recognition can be seen as a call to that recognition; this is Matthew's interpretation. Having regard to the group for whom he is writing, Matthew wants to confess his faith in the Son of God. In a more pragmatic perspective such as this, which could be further extended by analysis of the given material and ideological elements of any human community, the text demands a response from the reader or the hearer and thus moves closer to us.

Linguistics, like any science (historico-critical or otherwise), creates a sense of distance, sets things in order, using, as a means, the tools proper to reasoning. The intuitive element, in the sense of the 'intellectus' of the middle ages, the task of appropriation and personal involvement, does not, by hypothesis, take first place. This is why it may be useful, finally, to recall that the rational approach of linguists or philologists is only a move towards the profound heremeneutics of a text which appeals to faith. The 'world' of the Bible, and of Mark 6:45-53 and parallels in particular, must come and encounter 'my own world', in order to question it and to be questioned by it. The laborious analyses of exegetical scholars are merely a prelude to the task of personal understanding.

Translated by Christine Halek

Notes

1. G. Mounin *Clefs pour la linguistique* (Paris 1968) p. 23. See also, by the same aūthor, *Histoire de la linguistique des origines au XXe siècle* (Paris 1970²) and *La Linguistique du XXe siècle* (Paris 1975²).

2. See my introductory article, with its relevant bibliographical references: 'Die Bedeutung der modernen Linguistik für die Auslegung biblischer Texte' *Theologische Zeitschrift* 30 (1974) 223 -233.

3. N. Troubetzkoy *Principes de phonologie* (Paris 1949) p. 12.

4. For a presentation of this, see E. Gülich & W. Raible *Linguistische Textmodelle* (Munich 1977) pp. 280-305.

5. See also my article 'Analyse sémiotique et commentaire. Quelques réflexions à propos d'études de Luc 10:25-37' *New Testament Studies* 25 (1979) 454-468 (in particular p. 461f.). In this connection, we must not forget the contributions of scholars from Czechoslovakia, Russia and Scandinavia.

6. J. Barr *The Semantics of Biblical Language* (Oxford 1961).

7. In this connection, see my essay in a scholastic text-book: *Nytestamentlig teologi* (Lund 1979²).

8. See the presentation of the Nida-Taber method in B. Olsson *Structure and Meaning in the Fourth Gospel* (Lund 1974) (in particular p. 13f.).

9. In English translations, the connection between these two verses may seem less clear. The French version used in the original article makes it explicit, however: (v. 45 'lui-même renvoyait la foule'; v. 46 'après l'avoir congédiée'). (Translator's note.)

10. See P. Benoit and M.-E. Boismard *Synopse des quatre Évangiles en français* (Paris 1972) II p. 223.

11. Like John and Matthew, Mark uses *thalassa*, the 'sea', whereas Luke, in a different context, regains a sense of proportion by speaking of the 'lake' of Gennesaret (limnè).

12. The words 'estrangement' and 'union', used as opposites, translate *disjonction* and *conjunction*. Further on in the text, with reference to note 17, a more literal translation is given, in order to correspond with the presentation of the 'semiotic square'. (Translator's note)

13. E. Lohmeyer *Das Evangelium des Markus* (Göttingen 1937) p. 131ff.

14. W. Pesch *Das Markusevangelium* (Frieburg im Breisgau—Basle—Vienna 1977²) Part I p. 358.

15. This is set out in Groupe d'Entrevernes *Analyse sémiotique des textes* (Paris 1979); see also two analyses of our text in Groupe d'Entrevernes *Signes et paraboles. Sémiotique et texte évangélique* (Paris 1977) pp. 53-91, and J. Delorme 'L'intégration des petites unités littéraires dans l'Évangile de Marc du point de vue de la sémiotique structurale' *New Testament Studies* 25 (1979) 469-491 (especially 470-480). The review *Sémiotique et Bible* edited by the CADIR in Lyons, continues semiotic study along the lines pursued by Greimas.

16. The author is able to make use of the wider semantic field of the French *ciel* in relation to English, which must choose either 'sky' or 'heaven' as appropriate. (Translator's note)

17. The following 'semiotic square' may be constructed:

18. See my article referred to in note 5 above. Having completed that article, I read with interest a linguistic presentation of Mark 6:45-52 which agrees in part with my analysis: H. Ritt 'Der "Seewandel Jesu" (Mark 6:45-52 par)' *Biblische Zeitschrift* N.F.23 (1979) 71-84.

Fernando Belo

Why a Materialist Reading?

1. MATERIALIST READING

LET US first explain the words which shock when attached to the gospel.

Reading implies a semiotics, in this case that of Roland Barthes in his inimitable *S/Z*.[1] It has been called an admission of the lack of maturity of current work in semiotics, that of Greimas' school in particular, that it seeks to go beyond reading for the sake of reading, but *S/Z* also appeals to the intuition and passion of the reader when erudite patience is no longer or not yet convincing. Barthes' aim is no longer a 'science of narrative', but a reading of the specificity of a single narrative, in this case, the way in which Mark differs from the other gospels and should not be read as a synoptic variant. The difficulty, felt by some who have made attempts at a materialist reading of other biblical texts, is that 'my' reading remains in some sense too personal and difficult to transpose.

Materialist implies an epistemology, here that of the historical materialism deriving from Karl Marx, but broadened to take account of new questions, that of bodies and their desires in the symbolic networks of relationships, and that of texts and their codes as products of an economic-political-ideological formation.

This link between reading and historical materialism points up the difference from other, more scientific, more institutionalised methods which have been accepted because they have become, or are quickly becoming, fashionable. 'Reading' is in contrast to historico-critical exegesis because this latter lacks a theory of the text. 'Historical' contrasts with Greimas' structural analysis which wants nothing to do with history and delights in pure textual immanence. Of course, what we read is a narrative and not a history, but it is necessary, as a second stage, to consider the interaction between the text and the social formation in which it was produced. 'Materialist', which denotes the theoretical perspective of this consideration, is thus contrasted simultaneously with two other methods. The concept of the code is the key: as a narrative code, it does not leave the immanence of language, knows nothing of the author or of the events reported; as a code of the social formation, in close association with economics and politics, it makes it possible to take account of the effect of that social formation (class divisions and class struggles, for example) in the detail of the text itself.

'Materialist', by allowing on principle for the distance between the writings and readings of 1900 years ago and our own today, should make it possible to reach for the first time an ecclesiological proposition in which our practices, within a private capitalist or state capitalist industrial bureaucratic society, can find the place where they engage with a reading of the gospel, with the announcement of the resurrection in messianic power.

2. THE PERICOPE OF THE WALKING ON THE WATER AND CODES

Since space is limited, the reading will inevitably be schematic.[2] A narrative is a succession of sequences determined by its successivity. Dividing Mark into sequences produces a total of 73, of which the walking on the water is number 33. What makes it difficult to write an article like this, which sets out to illustrate the procedure in a particular sequence, is that this is just what is no longer possible once the text has been defined as a whole structured in such a way that each element, and so each sequence, can be read only in its relation to all the other elements, all the other sequences. Reading Mark therefore means first locating the different codes which run through the text as a whole and then trying to articulate them in relation to each other, being aware all the time that a number of attempts to read the text are possible and that there always remains an area of individual freedom in a reading which is decisive, while also making possible a polemic with other readings and other methods.

The various actors and their acts define the action code (here: Jesus sees, the disciples row, Jesus comes, etc.) and interact with each other in a system of relations. In the course of the narrative this system contrasts Jesus with the crowd (which looks for him, surrounds him, asks him for healings, acclaims him, etc.), with Opponents (who question him, try to destroy him and finally succeed), Individuals (who ask him for healings or challenged him), and disciples (who follow him and gradually separate out from the crowd), Twelve of whom will be clearly marked out until they finally perform healings themselves. The traitor, for example, will be defined semiotically by a change of role: from being 'one of the Twelve' he will become an Opponent.

The topographical code (in the case, mountain, sea, land) is defined primarily by the opposition between the town (with its distinctive sites, synagogue, house and temple) and outside-the-town (the location of the elements of this sequence). Its extension is the geographical code (here Bethsaida and Gennesaret), which contrasts Galilee, Judea and pagan countries.

These two codes engage with another, the strategic code, which defines the actors by their reciprocal strategies: Jesus chooses houses, the boat (here) and outside the town as a refuge where he is alone with his disciples, whereas the confrontations with Opponents almost always take place in the town, in the synagogue or in the temple, in the presence of the crowd, which supports him (except at the end in the presence of Pilate, where it changes strategy) and often follows him out of the town, to the lakeside. Jesus' miracle working will operate exclusively in Galilee, with three exceptions in pagan territory and one in Judea: it belongs to the symbolic code which relates to the body (which gets up, moves, touches, eats, etc.); in this case the walking on the water. The water, with the sky and the earth, forms part of the mythological code. This makes distinctions between the god and his voices, unclean spirits and men, and in it the mountain is a place particularly close to the god, the place where the prayer in our sequence takes place.

The analytic code structures the questions and answers relating to Jesus: Who is this man? What power has he? This code interacts with others in so far as Jesus eventually speaks to the crowd only in parables and keeps his gradual explanation of his teaching for the disciples alone. The analytic method used by Jesus consists in providing his activity as a key to a reading and leaving it to others to find the right answers to the questions. Neither voices from heaven nor those of unclean spirits are admitted by the narrative (demythologisation begins in Mark), nor are those of other actors (John the Baptist, Elijah, Satan, the lunatics, etc.). Only Peter succeeds in saying, 'You are the Messiah,' a title Jesus assumes later before the Sanhedrin.

The kingdom code structures the elements connected with the space of the 'circle on the way' (here the boat) which Jesus' strategy carves out of the space of social power. The whole of the social formation is controlled by this code, which is itself a social code, where we find, for example, our information about Jesus' family, his carpenter's trade, and his fishermen disciples (implied here by the boat) and the connotations of wealth, of the scribes' knowledge, etc. The internal articulation of the social code is constituted by the class difference between Jesus and those who follow him into the kingdom space, on the one hand, and his Opponents, on the other hand. This is decisive for entry into what he calls the kingdom of God, a space without rich, without lords, without scribes or other masters.

A final element to be noted is the level narrator/readers, where it is possible to find the narrator in the act of creating the narrative he gives the readers to read (they are mentioned in 6:13-14 and in our sequence in the final comment: 'for they did not understand about the loaves, but their hearts were hardened' (6:52)).

3. THE MATERIALIST MEANING OF MARK 6:45-52

(a) The Loaves and the Messiah

The seventy-three sequences of Mark combine into a few large sequences. Our present one forms part of the sequence of the loaves (6:30-8:30), which is distinct from those which precede it (the previous sequence, of the frequent journeys in Galilee, ends with the sending out of the Twelve) and those which follow it (which begin with the journey up to Jerusalem). It thus has the status of a strategic pause between Galilee and Judea: what is Jesus waiting for as he makes these boat trips from one side of the lake to the other? One striking feature is that it is the sequence of the loaves feeding the crowd in the wilderness, to which the narrator's comment refers here, which provides the key to this pause and another is that this story of loaves was imposed on Jesus by the crowd itself, by its strategy of pursuing him when he wanted rest. This long sequence is punctuated by comments on the hard hearts of the disciples, who do not understand what has just happened in the wilderness. In my reading I have attempted to show how Peter's reply in 8:29, which upsets the whole narrative, should be understood as the decipherment of the 'multiplications of loaves' as messianic, in the sense that they illustrate the fulfilment of the promise made to Israel that the poor would be filled according to the logic of the gift/debt system of the old Jewish symbolic order. We can deduce from this that the logic of the economic ideology of the dominant power closes hearts to an understanding of this crucial economic feature of Jewish messianism.[3]

(b) Messianism and Theology

I shall return to the sea sequence, but it would be frustrating for readers if I did not also give here details of some of the results of my reading of Mark as a whole.

Uncovering the level narrator/readers has enabled me to find a contradiction operating in the gospel text which has had enormous consequences in the history of Christianity. In Mark there is a narrative logic, connected with the strategic and analytic codes, which implies that Jesus himself did not foresee the end of the story (his death and resurrection),[4] but had a strategy for avoiding death and escaping to the pagan countries through Galilee. However, this logic is contradicted by a number of parenthetical comments in which Jesus announces his death and resurrection 'according

ures'; these announcements belong to the level of the narrator (who
he end of the story) and engender theological discourse. A symptomal
he style of Althusser enables us to restore the narrative, which has been
partially erased by this theological process, and to determine the reasons for the
erasure. It turns out to be connected with a strategic confrontation between Jesus and
the Zealots which runs as a fine thread through the narrative, and which also involves
the disciples. Mark, writing after the destruction of the Temple by the Romans,
compares the two failures (the cross and the defeat of 70) to the advantage of Jesus, who
has been proclaimed risen and constantly about to come in the glory of realised
eschatology. Theological discourse is at work here, playing the apologetic card, creating
an imaginary, sacrifical Christological space in which a new ecclesiastical priesthood will
in due course establish itself. There follows a wrong-headed reading of the gospels and
the Bible, interrupted here and there by protest movements of a more or less
millenarian type which spring up on the fringe of the churches and are denounced by
these as heretical.

(c) The Son of Man

How are we to assess this mysterious figure, so soon to disappear from the New
Testament? What is his status in Mark? Bultmann distinguished three sorts of texts
referring to the Son of Man, those mentioning him in terms of glory (9:1; 13:26; 14:62),
those which talk about the necessity of his suffering (8:31; 9:9; 9:31; 10:33; 10:45;
14:41), and lastly those referring to Jesus' activity before Peter's confession (2:10; 2:28).
I have tried to show how the first set are associated with a collective figure 'going'
towards heaven and the second, through a retroactive narrative effect of the
resurrection, individualise this figure in Jesus alone (an effect which, in reading, also
affects the first set). Since I said nothing in that discussion about the third group, I would
like to say something about it here. In these texts we can see the powerful praxis of Jesus
'contaminating' the paralytic who gets up in the same way that power goes out of him in
5:35 to cure the woman with the issue of blood: it is as though Jesus' activity created a
'powerful circle' round him. The Twelve become powerful in their turn; it is a sort of
collective which can even be subversive, since in 2:28 it is not certain that 'Son of Man'
does not refer *also* to the disciples, given that it is they who have just broken the sabbath,
and not Jesus. If this is right, we have a mysterious Son of Man whom Jesus in some way
brings into being around him, marking out the 'circle on the way' of those who would
have gone up to heaven in the way described in 1 Thess. 4:17 if there had been no death
and resurrection. Following the death and resurrection, theology individualised this
figure in Jesus alone, who was to 'come' from heaven, but at the messianic level it should
be read as the specific effect of Jesus' activity; his body was replaced at the last supper by
the practice of distributing loaves to satisfy hunger: 'this is my body'. This hypothesis
should be compared with Paul's idea of the body of Christ, which replaces the Son of
Man and has nothing to do with Pius XII's 'mystical body' since it is quite visible in its
effects, which liberate the body from oppression and encourage subversion.

(d) Fear and faith

Back to our sequence. The disciples' hearts are closed. They have understood
nothing about the loaves. And yet they had already shared Jesus' power. There was
therefore a new obstacle in the case of the loaves: what was it? It is that the little one has
one must give completely. In the same way we later find them astounded in the
discussion which follows the rich man's departure (10:17-31): Jesus has to take the risk
of a confrontation in Jerusalem, take up his cross: in short, losing one's life is the

condition of salvation. The reason for their failure to understand is that they are frightened. Anxiety and fear are certainly in evidence in the boat as they wear themselves out rowing against a contrary wind.[5] The exorcism of 4:39 implies that the sea is the domain of Satan. The Messiah, however ('It is I; have no fear'), walks on the sea; power makes him light. Fear, on the other hand, leads to sinking (Peter sinks in Matthew), makes people heavy, with the weight of acquired security, wealth and knowledge. The position of this sequence, then, after the sequence of the loaves, is perhaps to indicate that in the logic of the gospel 'giving' makes the givers light, eventually enabling them to walk on the sea and removing their fear. Fear, not error and not doubt, turns out to be the opposite of faith.

(e) Power and Us

The paradox of my materialist reading is, then, that it takes 'miracles' seriously, in complete contrast to modern exegesis. The problem has been that idealism, in its modern rationalist version, has been opposed to bodies and their power, even though Spinoza was moved to say, in a reference to sleep-walking, 'We do not even know what a body can do'. This would not perhaps be a 'miracle' in the modern pejorative sense stemming from our impotence as disembodied intellectuals. To quote Herberto Helder, a modern Portuguese poet, 'é sempre fácil caminhar en cima das aguas mas é imposível faże-lo miraculosamente' ('It is always easy to walk on the waters, but it is impossible to do it miraculously').

Demythologising, in idealist exegesis, is an operation in the head which ignores bodies; in contrast, materialist exegesis will produce results only if it enables bodies to get up and to walk on the waters, finally lightened by the removal of the weight of our pockets and our reasons. We have to read this power of which Mark gives us this astonishing story, read it to let it work on our bodies: that is where the Spirit will be (that is where my 'problems of faith' are). For this the text of the gospel must be liberated, liberated from its revealed truth, from its divine meaning, from its heavenly or demonic voices, from everything which overfills it; it must be, as it were, emptied. The meaning will then have to be looked for, not in the text but as a reading grid, in its articulation, in our bodily activities: the meaning will be the power which works on us, our bodies and our desires. It is theology which produces textual meaning, and demythologisation is reducing this theological element as a way of opening up our bodies. With open gospel, heart-bodies open, this is how Mark appears to me: it is an amazing text, a lion of a text.

And now a note by way of self-criticism. In 1974 I spoke as though the gospel could help us to make the revolution, but now things have changed. This is, alas, for me, the lesson of Portugal and Chile before it. But on the other hand there is perhaps another lesson for us there; that experience can perhaps teach us to make the earth ecological, powerful, to make it an earth where our bodies and the bodies of our children can work, function, produce (instead of labouring on the production lines of factories and offices), and dance and play. Maybe like children playing the flute in the market-place (Luke 7.32)?

4. EXEGESIS AND LINGUISTIC PHILOSOPHY

This article upsets me: through wanting to say too much in too short a space it has sacrificed beauty. And yet I cannot avoid adding a few remarks about the lack of critical attention paid by exegetes, with a few exceptions, to the more or less empiricist, more or less 'Greek', but always idealist, philosophies which operate, unknown to them, in their arguments. My remarks concern what seems to me to be the dominant semiotic character of the biblical texts,[6] in contrast to the dominant character of the Greek philosophical texts which have determined the arguments of western theology, exegesis included.

As I see it, in the Bible narrative is more important than gnoseology. Verbs of action are strong, and articulate temporality around 'event' (action, activity). In their predication, in the strict grammatical sense of the term, they proclaim extralinguistic reality as transformation, metamorphosis. In direct contrast, Greek philosophy turns on the copula 'is' as the degree zero of predication. Reality is understood as substance (nouns are more important than verbs) and temporality tends to be absorbed into a gnoseological atemporal present. The Logos in the Bible (in Mark at least) is action, activity, with a unique story, the opposite of the more or less eternal truth of Greco-Christian theology.

The most important feature of biblical thought is not concept or essence, but much more metonymy and metaphor. Metonymy is 'material': for example, the vine, the flock, the fig tree, the harvest, are figures of Israel, which is being understood, therefore, in terms of its economic activity. The spirit is breath and wind, forces which lead to action, never presence, temple *theo-ory* (which is contemplation, according to Heidegger). Subsequently metaphor combines series of metonymies by comparing different actions and different narratives. The finest example is the parables, which are typical of a form of reasoning which never presses towards Greek abstraction or systematisation, but prefers to keep to a fragmentary form of gnoseology as exemplified by the proverbs, the various types of commentary called midrash, etc.

A corollary of this semiotics is that the crucial feature of biblical language is its view of the logos and the spirit as creative,[7] life-giving: the fruitfulness of the earth, of females, of women: life is exuberance, overflow, the multiplication of fruits, fulness, blessing. The Hebrews, with the exception of the priests, must be imagined as active, transformers, enthusiasts for metamorphosis—perhaps this is what peace, justice and grace are—driven by an abhorrence of death, that curse. The two conceptions of desire in the Bible are opposed in the same way as covetousness and power, debt and gift.

If this is really true, while Marx and Freud are a help in materialist readings of the Bible, they can only take us so far, for they remain very Greek. It is Nietzsche, that anti-Socratic and anti-Christ who is best able to help our eyes and our bodies rediscover evangelical power. Leaving aside questions of sense and spirituality, of the immortality of the soul, we begin then to understand that it is the resurrection, such an embarrassing subject for theologians descended from the Greeks, which is no less than the touchstone of a reading of the Bible in terms of power. God is not the 'explanation' of power; the unprecedented metamorphosis of bodies to form an ecclesial network can be announced as a resurrection through the power which works on those bodies. All we shall know of God is this seed. Our understanding of the figure of the Son of Man now must be ecological: he must be the fruit of the earth.

Translated from the French by Francis McDonagh

Notes

1. R. Barthes *S/Z* (London 1975).

2. This article does not argue the case. For arguments, see F. Belo *Lecture matérialiste de l'évangile de Marc* (Paris 1974), now available in an American edition (1980), and F. Belo *La Puissance des corps. Où va la lecture matérialiste de l'évangile de Marc?* (Paris, forthcoming).

3. I have often been accused of reductionism, and this is my opportunity to put the ball in my opponents' court. Is not a failure to understand this economic determination of the messianism of the gospel on the part of theologians, bishops and exegetes the source of a much more dangerous reductionism?

4. See the little parable, 4:26-29, which has disappeared from the other Synoptics. Applied to Jesus as the peasant who sows, it says that he 'knows not how' the fruit comes or fails to come.

5. Fear is often involved in Mark's description of the disciples' failure to understand; it is even his last word (16:8).

6. I am talking about semiotics, which is concerned with texts, and not about linguistics, which is concerned with the Hebrew language, where my incompetence is total.

7. 'With us saying and doing share a table,' says the French Jewish poet H. Meschonnic, nicely.

Dominique Stein

Is a Psycho-Analytical Reading of the Bible Possible?

THE CHOICE of Mark 6:45-52 is an excellent one: it presents obvious difficulties and it allows no scope for the crudest trap into which I could fall, that of a psychologising interpretation. Before tackling the question of the legitimacy of a psycho-analytical reading of the Bible, I need to indicate a few axes of possible different interpretations.

If we take this text in isolation, it opens and closes enigmatically: at the beginning, Jesus 'made' his disciples (get into the boat). We are nowhere told where this obligation came from. Is he opposing some refusal, some resistance on the part of the disciples? Is he responding to some urgency about the destination of the journey? Does it correspond to a secret purpose and, if so, what? The concluding phrase is no less astonishing: 'they did not understand about the loaves, but their hearts were hardened.' Since this pericope does not mention the incident of the loaves, either we shall never know about it, or else it is related elsewhere in Mark so that we have to reread the whole passage in a different light, in its context.

For the time being, however, let us remain within the limits of the verses put to us. The title usually given is ambiguous; and Jesus's walking on the water is in fact framed by two phrases which supply its motivation: 'they were distressed in rowing, for the wind was against them' and 'the wind ceased'. At the very least, therefore, we should give it another title: Jesus walks on the waters *and* calms the sea by his presence alone.

The spatial theme can be read along various axes of reference: the opposition of verticality/horizontality (hill/sea, walking upright/disciples in the boat), the opposition of nearness/distance (going before him to the other shore/leaving in order to pray, boat on the sea/he alone on the land, coming towards them/passing by them/getting into the boat with them).

We may also note the way in which the narrative is punctuated temporally: 'immediately', 'while', 'after', 'when evening came', 'about the fourth watch of the night'. The adjectives denoting affect are potent: 'alone', 'distressed', 'terrified', 'hardened'. Looking at this passage symbolically, the sea that violently separates Jesus from his disciples at the beginning becomes a path of reunion in v. 48, sea and land becoming one under the feet of Jesus. From a literary point of view we have not only to note the dramatic crescendo of the narrative but to situate it in the genre of a miracle story, albeit with the qualification that two different prodigies are in question, concerned with the reversal of the laws of nature (walking on the water) and the mastery

24

of these laws (calming the wind), prodigies that here involve Jesus alone and his relationship with the disciples. The central term 'ghost' deserves special treatment, to which I shall return.

The attempt to reinsert these verses into the continuum of Mark's gospel as a whole immediately and minimally raises the question of the relationship to the preceding story of the feeding of the crowd and to the following verse (v. 53) which makes v. 52 less obscure but at the cost of contradicting v. 45, the importance of which, in its very dissonance, would justify considering it on its own, either in the perspective of a symbolic geography, or as part of a study of different redactional sources. A comparison of parallel versions reveals differences that make the text fall apart. To cite only a few: in Matthew's text Peter in his turn walks on the water and the story closes with a confession of faith. In John's version, Jesus's withdrawal to the mountains has connotations of the recognition of his messianic mission. Mark's account is the only one to bring out the topographic discordance (Bethsaida-Gennesaret) and above all the fact that 'they did not understand'. . . .

As the reader will have seen for himself, the bird's eye view of the text which I have just taken has strictly nothing particularly psycho-analytical about it; it goes to show only how one might set about placing marker buoys and the almost limitless levels of analysis.

1. WHAT PSYCHO-ANALYTICAL READINGS OF THE BIBLE USUALLY ARE

(a) *Some Presuppositions*

Those who have gone about the psycho-analytical reading of the biblical texts agree on certain negative principles: the fact that the text studied has to be taken in its entirety, like the manifest content of a dream, does not mean that one then has to go about extracting some would-be latent content as if one were winkling out an insect from under a stone. And when one is dealing with a first-person narrative as in the case of the letters of St Paul it is no more a question of playing the apostle's psycho-analyst or of purporting to sketch his psychological portrait.[1]

On the basis of the understanding of man presupposed by the corpus of its concepts, a psycho-analytical reading would (and I say 'would' advisedly) consist in an attentive reading of, in the first place, the gaps, the discordances, the slips in the texts, deemed to be as significant as the avowed message.[2] By the same token, it would also be a reading that is particularly attentive to symbolic representations reminiscent of the unconscious symbolic representations the emergence of which in dreams, symptoms or fantasies allows them to be elucidated.

More radically, a psycho-analytical reading would bring a meaning to light: 'Something becomes significant when it discloses a hole in received habits of thinking and common speech and flowers into questions and meanings. This is what Scripture does in so far as it has never ceased to give people pause to think, speak and write since it was put down. . . . The work of analysis consists not in disengaging the hidden significance of a manifest content but in disclosing in history what is being said there about the relationship to meaning, of the place of the death and effacement of the speaking subject, and of the mechanism of distortion. . . . We have to wait for the accounts of the passion and resurrection in order to have it said that the death and effacement concern the speaking subject himself and in order to have what sustains Scripture and its meaning presented in a content.'[3]

c

(b) *The direction of a psycho-analytical reading of Mark 6:45-53*

On the basis of such presuppositions, then, what direction would the reading of Mark 6:45-53 take?

(i) If we want to begin by dwelling on the discordances of the text, we should note that v. 52 sends us back to the account of the feeding of the five thousand. The disciples' failure to understand and their passivity ('made' as they were to get into the boat) is of a piece with their failure to understand what Jesus wanted to do for the crowd (not to bring bread but to feed them gratis) and is opposed to their role of active intermediaries between Jesus and the crowd. It is true that it is not they who say the blessing, but it is to them that the gifts are handed over so that they can 'set them before the people'. They are displaced subjects, subjects who do not speak, but they are subjects all the same. In this perspective of the tension between speaking and dumb subject, we could return to the passage and now read, on the one hand: 'they cried out', on the other, 'he spoke to them and said'—an opposition between the infant, the *infans*, and him who says 'I', who says 'It is I': you exist only to the extent that I name you, my word is performative, it is I who constitute your desire by displacing it, by assigning it a place where you did not know it was ('He meant to pass by them').

(ii) If we prefer to dwell on the symbolic light, our text becomes inexhaustibly rich. The sea that within the space of a walk becomes solid land takes us back to the most ancient and fruitful myths of the nourishing Earth: the Earth-mother from which all life surges—unless it becomes a mortal trap, a trap in which Peter does not fail to be swallowed up in the Matthean version.[4] It is a death-dealing Mother unless the word of the Other 'take heart, it is I' (in Matthew's version, it is a question: 'Why did you doubt?') intervenes to re-establish the subject as the subject of his own words in face of the mystery of the anguishing pit of non-saying, non-knowing, of desire without a law that it at one and the same time constitutive and prohibiting.

I had put on one side the status of the significant 'ghost' ('they thought it was a ghost, and cried out'). This ghost introduces a twofold theme: that of corporality and that of a transcorporality that is at the opposite pole to a non-corporality considered to be dangerous, demonic. Yet the 'It is I', absolute sign of transcendence, cannot manifest itself in an incorporeal demon. All the accounts of the post-Easter appearances come surging in at this point, giving the prodigious incident its true dimension: It is I, it is not an incorporeal demon, a fairy appearance, no, I am going beyond you, just as I shall be preceding you later, just as I make deliberate choice of you as subjects of the word to come, despite—or because of—your disturbance. In the measure of the very hardness (of your resistance), of your failure to understand (your denial tied to your repression), I am installing you in the order of confidence, for it is indeed I—my living body—who am near you, and not the lethal fantasy of an hallucination. It is because it is I and because it is you that a future opens up. But you see that it will come about only through tempest and anguish, and that I shall have to pass beyond you in order to rejoin you: This is the way in which what L. Beirnaert suggested was the point of a psycho-analytical reading could be read in the text as it were in filigree, namely, the death and effacement of the speaking subject himself in the face of the passion and resurrection to come.[5]

(iii) If I have elected to use a conceptual apparatus in which need, demand, desire, the reference to the Other and to the Subject of desire, lack and its function are the primary points of reference, this is because most French-speaking analysts who have devoted themselves to a reading of the Bible operate implicitly or explicitly within the universe of discourse of Jacques Lacan. It goes without saying that the same procedure could make use of a terminology nearer the classical terminology of Freud (as is evidenced by the recurrence of such terms as resistance, denial, repression). Thus Jesus's walking on the water in order to rejoin and pass beyond his disciples would be part of the dramatic configuration of the situation of Oedipus: is it not necessary that the subject (= the disciples) in the repression of his desire for the mother (the nourisher: 'they did not understand about the loaves') has to live through his anguish, an anguish that suggests some return of the repressed, an anguish partially relieved by the father's word ('Take heart, it is I; have no fear'), a father who rises in order to forbid him the mother (= the sea, the water of birth and life, source of nourishment, of fish). Peter experiences this cruelly in Matthew's version where the sea becomes close (there is no longer any separation between sea and land) but is reserved for the father (Matthew 14:22-33).

Such, then, are the axes of reference, with their terminological variants and differences of perspective, according to which a psycho-analytical reading of a biblical text could be conducted. The reader will no doubt regret that I have done no more than outline the different ways of carrying such a reading through. Above all I do hope that he will have been struck by what I shall roundly call a veritable *methodological swindle*.

2. THE METHODOLOGICAL VICE OF SUCH FORMS OF READING

What I claim is that the readings I have sketched, far from opening up the text, close it. If we look at it a little more closely, we see that the concepts I have used—and it does not matter whether they derive from Freud or from Lacan—function as garments which clothe and disguise the text, whilst claiming to say more, to reveal the hidden meaning. If I may use a crude simile, I should say that this sort of pseudo-analysis is like a canning factory: if you put pigs in at one end, you will have tinned pork at the other, albeit in a different form, but in any case (subject to gross fraud!) only what is in the pigs. Similarly, the terms borrowed from psycho-analytical theory, which in reality amount only to a paraphrase, reveal nothing new. The most they do is to serve as an illustration of the way in which what Freud had already discovered can be disclosed again in this particular text.

Does the reading of the New Testament get any further illumination through thinking of the disciples as actors in the oedipal drama? It may well be that we can see this scene unfold in terms of a demand, a need, a desire (which is the way in which some psycho-analysts see every relationship between subject and object). But does this pericope of the gospel gain anything through being read in this light? Ever since Freud wrote *The Interpretation of Dreams*, who does not know that every man is, in his dreams, master of the elements, conqueror of time and space? But do we have to recall this every time we read an account of some miraculous happening? Many 'psycho-analytic' readings, whether of the Old or the New Testament, come down to being an application (in the sense in which we say we *apply* a dressing) of a pre-established grill familiar to the author on—not to—a text which serves more as a proof than as object of study.

It could at this point be objected that this is what Freud himself did. Did he not, in *Moses and Monotheism*, *Leonardo da Vinci and a Memory of His Childhood*, blaze the trail for what was soon called applied psycho-analysis? We have to remember that Freud and the first generation of psycho-analysts who followed him in this respect were more concerned to find confirmation of their intuitions in culture than to astound their contemporaries by stigmatising Hamlet as the prototype of the man who had been made ill by his oedipal conflicts. To begin with, the so-called works of 'applied psycho-analysis' had a twofold purpose; on the one hand, to touch the detractors of psycho-analysis by showing them that the common stock of western culture is packed with examples that converge on Freud's discoveries about the unconscious, and, on the other hand, to allow authors, through a re-reading of influential works, to find encouragement for their intuitions and to retrace their own history by interpreting that of others. Freud's *Moses and Monotheism* sets the pace in this regard. This is no longer where we are now. This is why I am being asked to respond to the question that is ours today: can psycho-analysis help us to understand a text, and especially a biblical text? Before setting about a reply, I should like to clear psycho-analytic readings of a certain number of accusations.

3. THE INVALIDITY OF CERTAIN OBJECTIONS MADE AGAINST THE PSYCHO-ANALYTIC
READING OF THE BIBLE

(a) *Reductive?*

The first and most common head of indictment concerns the interpretation: it is accused of being *reductive*. This complaint is so common that authors defend themselves against it themselves (see note 1). As M. Sales writes: 'The thorniest problem about readings of the Bible that claim to be psycho-analytic arises wherever it is impossible to avoid quite explicitly theological meanings. . . . This is particularly the case for the whole of the New Testament and especially the gospels. Here the text is such that anybody who does not accept its cutting edge is forced to deflect it by a massive reduction of the central message which it contains . . .'.[6]

We should at this point perhaps recall that the (very complex) status of interpretation in the practice of psycho-analysis forbids us to designate it as reductive on the ground that this is a contradiction in terms: either interpretation yields a new meaning, or else it is not interpretation. We do, however, in fairness also have to add that such a verification can occur only after the event, by seeing whether the interpretation has in fact effected a change of understanding, a displacement, the removal of an inhibition. Besides which, the very use of the epithet 'reductive' is instinct with the repugnance so many—and particularly clerical—commentators have about bringing together psycho-analysis, mustily redolent of sexuality as it is, and sacred wit.

(b) *Over-clinical?*

A second sort of criticism is tied to a certain conception of psycho-analytic reading: such a reading seems to be clinical, the sort of thing one would expect to find in a text-book of symptoms such as pathology deals with, and therefore to be understood in other terms of reference which underlie the manifest text. This is why we have to be careful how we set about the reading of any given short passage: 'What gives a diagnosis value in psycho-analysis is the number of observations: one needs time to unlock an individual's unconscious mechanisms. This is why it is by extending the hypothesis of an interpretation of any given particular passage to the whole corpus that it becomes possible to make a pronouncement about the structure of the "other system" of which the entire corpus is a trace.'[7] Such a criticism would be valid only to the extent that one accepted the conception of psycho-analysis on which it rests. I shall show later that I do not accept it.

(c) *Subjective?*

There is a third complaint and it is not the least one: the psycho-analytic reading is subjective, contingent, unrigorous. I want to come back to the function of the 'I' in any such subjectivity. But we have to remember that if any interpretation refused by the patient is not necessarily valid, the exclamation: 'Oh, but that's your interpretation' makes a psycho-analyst think that he is on the right track. The validity of an interpretation is to be judged according to the retrospective criteria which I mentioned above, but we also have to recall that is it a contingent construction (several interpretations would be possible, the moment and the formulation of this interpretation could have been different); but, once it has been uttered, it has the status of an act which can no longer be put in question.[8] Any subsequent interpretation on the same point can be made on this basis, however indefinite in character the overdetermination of the same production of the unconscious may be.

(d) Irrelevant?

The fourth and last complaint, which takes in the previous ones (and particularly the one about reductionism) is simply this: given the psycho-analytic reading can, by definition, apply to any text, it is, in the final analysis, unable to cope with what M. Sales called the cutting edge of the text (see note 6). As J.-N. Aletti puts it: 'What makes particular writings (the gospels) Writ (with a capital W), that is to say the reference of all Christian discourse, is the resurrection, condition and object of an act of faith. This is why the relationship between Holy Writ and writing cannot be analysed by the human sciences.'[7] And M. Sales writes a propos of Françoise Dolto's book (L'Evangile au risque de la psychanalyse[9]): 'The Gospel is not at much risk from such an undertaking which hardly serves Scripture and does not honour psycho-analysis.'

The upshot of these criticisms is to deprive psycho-analysis of the last word in regard to the canonical writings: psycho-analysis can indeed teach us some things but its limits forbid it to deal with the essential thing, namely, the relationship between the reading of Scripture and faith. It is inadequate to its object. Apart from the question of substance which I shall tackle by way of conclusion, these criticisms, which always come after praise of the historico-critical methods, are uncannily reminiscent of the anathemas hurled at the precursors of these same methods, which have now become classical. How fearful the guardians of the faith are!

4. WHAT A PSYCHO-ANALYTIC READING OF THE BIBLE COULD BE

So far, then, after running through Mark's text, I have sought to show what a psycho-analytic reading according to commonly accepted criteria would be like, once certain conditions were met (respect for the integrity of the text, refusal to seek out a supposedly latent content, not psychologising the actors in the story). I hope that I have succeeded in making it vividly obvious that such a would-be psycho-analytic reading is a snare and that a certain style of applied psycho-analysis is outworn.

As for the most common criticisms made of psycho-analytic readings, they rest on a misunderstanding. The inadequacy of a method of reading (the theoretical psycho-analytical corpus) to its object (Scripture) is not in question. What is in question is the definition of the criteria of validity of a psycho-analytic method of reading, and, even more, its application.

(a) Some Criteria of Validity

Too often either the definition given has nothing specific about it and could just as well apply to any other sort of reading (see Beirnaert's definition which I quoted above), or else the author does not carry out his own programme. Thus A. Vergote writes: 'To understand a text also involves understanding it for oneself, making the sense one's own.'[10] All he does in the rest of his study, however, is to grasp the structural homologies that there are between the structures of the unconscious and the Pauline texts. The author himself as the subject of his own reading disappears completely, he says nothing about any process triggered off in him, any resonance set in him by Paul's text.

This is where I see the major difficulty arise. It would be easy enough to come back at me and say: Alright then, you are not psycho-analysing Paul, Jesus or Peter, but in that case you are exposing your own psycho-analysis. Yes and no. What is in question here is the whole matter of the 'I' in psycho-analysis and the difference between the way it is deployed there and a debased subjectivism.

For I reject the application of a psycho-analytic grid to any text whatever, I think—contrary to the semiotician (see the admirable analysis of the passage we are discussing made by the Groupe d'Entrevernes[11]) who has a ready-made method which enables him to proceed to his reading—that the psycho-analyst has no 'method' at his disposition. What he has got is the experience of a procedure, a procedure which neither illustrates nor verifies a theory the data of which he has somehow mastered beforehand but which makes him discover, create, find from moment to moment what the theoretical corpus proposes to him.

Does this mean that the psycho-analyst had nothing to say about the texts of the Bible? If the question put is: Has exegesis anything to expect from psycho-analysis? my unhesitating reply is: No. *Exegesis has nothing to expect from psycho-analysis.* The psycho-analyst does, however, have something to expect from Scripture. Often it is something to read like anything else, the decipherment of one of the monuments of our culture in which psycho-analysis is rooted, and he will deploy what he has learned from his daily practice: attentive listening and, as far as possible, without prejudging the letter, the internal and external associations of the text, the attachment of the text to its context and its overarching end. This last point is worth stressing. It makes a nonsense of the criticism to the effect that the psycho-analyst is incompetent to deal with theological or other subject-matter and that he reduces things to their lowest common denominator. How would it be possible in Mark 6:45-52 to set aside, for instance, the terms referring directly to God or to the resurrection, when the text speaks implicitly about prayer and the fear of the disciples in the face of a body without a body, a phantom: such a putting aside would make the text literally senseless.

This sort of reading will, therefore, not have enriched the understanding of the text more than any other. We must, however, recall that a text without a reader has ceased to live. The theory of psycho-analysis may not have augmented. But if the psycho-analyst has really become involved with his reading, really made it his own, he will, in this rather exceptional way of reading it, have merged into what is most universal in psycho-analysis: the 'I'. He will have created a new work, subject to the consistence and demands of the text read, but new nevertheless. A particularly telling example of this recreation is to be found in the work which Conrad Stein has pursued for nearly twenty years in relation to Sigmund Freud's *The Interpretation of Dreams.*[12]

In other cases (and these constitute the majority of 'psycho-analytic readings' of the Bible) the psycho-analytic author speaks implicitly or explicitly as a believer, as a subject who makes an investment in the text concerned in a way that could hardly be described as neutral. Sometimes the mixture of the 'psycho-analytic' and 'Christian' types verges on incongruity: I have to admit that I could never have imagined that I should be offered a 'Christian way of resolving the Oedipus complex . . .'.[13]

(b) The Application

These extremes apart, I do not cease to be amazed that the authors who write about biblical texts with the greatest freedom, spontaneity and personal involvement (like

Françoise Dolto, in the book I have already cited) do not at the same time question their motivation in reading these texts, in other words, their relationship to the faith, the way their faith is integrated into their practice, their methodology, their psycho-analytic criticism. Finally, if a psycho-analytic cure is so often accused of causing people to 'lose their faith', this is not merely a chimera calculated to afford a defence to somebody fleeing the risks of a cure. The fact is that the practice of psycho-analysis and its commerce with the unconscious is a *critical* practice. So you are a psycho-analyst, you have the faith, you read the Bible. Very well, then, but can you tell us whether you have weighed up the advantages which this adherence brings you, the fears which it removes, the tendency to become identified with omnipotence which it subtends. I realise full well that it is almost impossibly difficult to do this. For every psycho-analyst has the experience that his desire to write aims simultaneously at removing and maintaining denial. But I should like the question to be at least put and the history of faith within each one of us to be at least evoked, as a process of which the subject must take account.

I can already feel the last and legitimate question coming: And what about you? This is a searing request which almost made me refuse to write this article. If there had not been so many misunderstandings about psycho-analytic readings of the Bible, if I were not convinced that we have both to stop expectations about psycho-analysis which it cannot fulfil and also to allow the psycho-analyst passionately devoted to reading the Bible a chance to speak, I should not have written the above pages. I should just have contented myself with saying: Leave me alone to read Mark as I am, let the text work in me, leave its indelible marks in me; help me see what has not been shown, hear what will not be said again, what will go on being said for ever, let me go along with him who did not understand. . . .

'He has pulled the boat up the shore. He looks at the tattered sail rather bleakly and estimates the time he will need to repair it. The harrowing day, the nightmarish night, had meant nothing to him. Everything had been forced on them, gone against them. He had no sooner settled down to take a well-earned rest than he had had to set off again. When the freshness of the evening was stealing into their soured clothes, he had to stay behind, and with all these people. Then what madness to embark at night when the wind was rising! Why? His bitterness dissolves into fatigue, his recollections become confused, he sees faces again.

He sees the face of that woman again when he had brought her bread yesterday. She had thanked him. Famished, yet not avid. Moved, without fear. (He is so frightened himself, deep down. He is so frightened tonight.) Patient, with an age-old patience, on the point of breaking out into a quite new impatience. Instinct with attention, and lovely from the harmony between her and the green grass, despite the dust and the noise. He is going to refind her. She will understand that he did not understand. She will understand that he understood, that he practically understood. She will come with them.

When the light makes the sea and the sand one single scintillating surface, he will wake up.'

Translated by John Maxwell

Notes

1. A. Vergote 'Apport des données psychanalytiques à l'exégèse' *Exégèse et herméneutique* (Paris 1971) 109-173.

2. A. Vergote 'Psychanalyse et interprétation biblique' *Dictionnaire de la Bible, Supplement* IX (1973-1975) 252-260.

3. L. Beirnaert 'Approche psychanalytique' *Les Miracles de Jésus* (Paris 1977) 183-188.

4. P. Benoit and M. E. Boismard *Synopse des quatre évangiles* II p. 449 on the theme of 'Peter's doctrine'.

5. L. Beirnaert 'La Violence homicide, l'histoire de Caïn et d'Abel' *Le Supplément* 119 (1976) 435-444.

6. M. Sales S.J. 'Possibilités et limites d'une lecture psych-analytique de la Bible *Nouvelle Revue Theologique* (1979) 699.

7. J. N. Aletti 'Une lecture en questions' *Les Miracles de Jesus* cited in note 3, 189-208.

8. On this theme, see, for example, S. Viderman *La Construction de l'espace analytique* (Paris 1970) pp. 55-71.

9. F. Dolto *L'Evangile au risque de la psychanalyse* (Paris 1977) I (1978) II.

10. A. Vergote 'Apport des données psychanalytiques à l'exégèse' cited in note 1.

11. *Signes et paraboles, Sémiotique et textes évangeliques* (Groupe d'Entrevernes), 'Ils n'avaient pas compris au sujet des pains' 53-91.

12. C. Stein 'Sur l'écriture de Freud' *Etudes Freudiennes* (Paris) No. 708, 70-119; L'Emergence, fragment d'un commentaire de L'Interprétation des rêves de S. Freud' Etudes Freudiennes (Paris) No. 9-10, 147-167; *La Mort d'Oedipe* (Paris 1977) and see in particular Ch. 4, pp. 75-92.

13. A. Besançon 'Du Modèle chrétien de résolution du complexe d'Oedipe' *Contrepoint* (Paris) No. 6 (1972) 79-94.

PART II

Practical Exegesis Today

Pinchas Lapide

A Jewish Exegesis of the Walking on the Water

1. JEWISH QUESTIONS

THE READER of St Mark's account of the walking on the water finds himself face to face with several questions and difficulties.

Why had Jesus to 'make' (6:45) his disciples get into the boat (a hapax legomenon in Mark)?

Does not the assertion that Jesus withdraws, as on so many other occasions, in order to 'pray' (6:46) in solitude, conflict with the view, common in later interpretations of the walking on the water, that the incident is to be regarded as a theophany?

If it was 'already very late' (6:35) before the feeding of the 'five thousand men' (6:44) began, how can the evangelist, describing what happened after they had been fed, the remains of the bread and fish collected, the crowd dismissed and the disciples sent away, continue: 'when evening came' (6:47)?

If the boat was 'in the middle of the sea' (which implies a distance of at least four kilometres from the shore), how could Jesus 'see' that they 'were distressed in rowing' (6:48)?

If he could see that they 'were distressed', why did Jesus wait from the 'evening' until daybreak ('the fourth watch') before he 'came to them' (6:48)?

Is his walking on the water remotely conceivable, in view of the strong 'contrary wind' (6:48) and the force of the waves?

How can the words 'he meant to pass them by' (6:48) be reconciled with his obvious intention to bring them help in their distress?

If the disciples saw 'him'—that is, Jesus—why did they 'think it was a ghost' (6:49)?

Why does the boat start out from the place of the feeding of the five thousand in the evening, to go, on Jesus' instructions, to Bethsaida (6:45), and arrive in broad daylight completely unexpectedly in Gennesaret (6:53)?

Since any Jew of that time, having just experienced the miracle of the feeding of the five thousand, would have had no difficulty in believing that Jesus, if he wanted, could also walk on the water, why all the 'crying out', 'terror' and 'confusion' (6:49f.) on the part of the disciples?

If the disciples had not understood 'about the loaves' (6:52), why is nothing said here

35

about the fish of the feeding miracle?

Exactly what did the disciples 'not understand' 'about the loaves' (6:52)?

Since Jews and Christians will certainly give different answers to these frank questions, we must have recourse to the rabbinical eschatological hope, expressed by the root TEKU, which says of disputed interpretations, 'the Tishbite (that is, Elijah of Tishbe, as forerunner of the Messiah) will answer all questions and problems'.[1]

2. THE PRE-MARCAN CORE

Whether this walking on the water was already linked with the feeding of the five thousand in the pre-Marcan tradition; whether Mark's intention was to present a 'nature-miracle', a 'sign of God's approval' of Jesus, an account of the stilling of a storm, christophany, a prefiguration of the eucharist, or a combination of these elements—such questions are still in dispute. So too is the basic question as to the extent of Mark's editorial activity, and as to what, if anything, can be regarded as the historical core of the narrative. To get back to the earliest tradition, obviously we should first discard those passages which clearly display the two well-known characteristics of Marcan editing: the so-called Messianic Secret and the disciples' failure to understand.

(a) Discarding the passages characteristic of Marcan editing

To the first belong, in my opinion, in the light of Mark 1:1, all those elements which would depict the walking on the water as a manifestation of 'the Son of God'. This would include the descent of Jesus 'from the mountain' (see Deut. 33:2; Judges 5:4f.; Hab. 3:3), and the fact that he treads on the water (see Ps. 77:19; Isa. 43:16; LXX Job 9:8).

On the one hand, there is a parallel with Moses, the 'first prophet' (Deut. 34:10), and with the prophets Elijah and Elisha, all of whom could walk dry-shod through the water: 'The Lord said to Moses. . . . "Lift up your rod, and stretch out your hand over the sea and divide it (in the *midst*) . . . that the people of Israel may go on dry ground through (the *midst* of) the sea". . . . And the people of Israel went into the *midst* of the sea. . . .' (Exod. 14:15f. and 22).

The threefold 'in the midst of the sea' or 'through the midst of the sea' may be echoed in Mark 6:47: 'in the middle of the sea'—especially in view of the fact that Moses is six times explicitly mentioned by Mark (Mark 1:44; 7:10; 10:3 and 4; 12:19; 12:26), and several other times seems to be present at the back of his mind as the one with whom Jesus is compared.

However, since the time was 'near to Passover', as John 6:4 explains, it may be that the original reference was to a verse in the Hallel Psalms, which are repeated on the evening of the Passover: 'When Israel went forth from Egypt . . . Judah became his sanctuary, Israel his dominion. The sea looked and fled. . . . What ails you, O sea, that you flee?' (Ps. 114:1ff.).

The parallel with Elijah and Elisha seems even clearer: 'Fifty men of the sons of the prophets also went, and stood at some distance from them, as they both were standing by the Jordan. Then Elijah took his mantle . . . and struck the water, and the water was parted to the one side and to the other, till the two of them could go over on dry ground' (2 Kings 2:7f.).

'Then he (Elisha) took the mantle of Elijah that had fallen from him, and struck the water, saying, "Where is the Lord, the God of Elijah?" And . . . the water was parted to the one side and to the other; and Elisha went over. . .' (2 Kings 2:14f.).

Since Moses and Elijah, who were only able to bring the waters under control by the help of God, are the chief witnesses at the transfiguration (Mark 9:4ff.), it may be that

Mark 6:48a rests on a pre-Marcan tradition which likens Jesus to these prophets. There is actually a double parallel—in the feeding miracle (compare 2 Kings 4:42-44 with Mark 6:35-44) as well as in the walking on the water (compare 2 Kings 2:14f. with Mark 6:45-52).

On the other hand, Mark 6:48b clearly shows the hand of Mark. The words 'he meant to pass by them' are intended to evoke the threefold 'passing by' of God and his goodness before Moses: 'I will make all my goodness *pass* before you, and will proclaim before you my name, "The Lord" . . . and while my glory *passes by* I will put you in a cleft of the rock, and I will cover you with my hand until I have *passed by* . . .' (Exod. 33:19-23).

The 'proclaiming of the name of the Lord' which is here promised to Moses may have pointed to the revelation-formula 'εσώ ἐιμί as we know it from Exodus 3:14, but only in the LXX translation. 'Passing by' *without* being recognised (Mark 6:49) could have been borrowed from the theophany in Job, where we read: 'Lo, he passes by me, and I see him not; he moves on, but I do not perceive him' (Job 9:11)—especially seeing that two verses earlier in Job it says: 'The Lord . . . trampled the waves of the sea' (Job 9:8). Similarly the fear-motif, expressed in the bewilderment, dread and terror of the disciples ('utterly astounded' in 51b), which, in the pericope we are studying, seems to be totally lacking in logic, can only have been taken from the 'flight' and 'fear' of the people (Exod. 20:18 and 20) in the LXX version of the theophany on Sinai—as must 'they were exceedingly afraid' (Mark 9:6), when Jesus was transfigured on 'a high mountain' (Mark 9:2).

'Have no fear' (6:50b) would, however, not then be a word of God, but rather would correspond to the calming of the people by Moses (Exod. 20:20), and would come close to one of the early Christian conceptions of Jesus as Moses Redivivus.[2]

So far as the second Marcan feature—the disciples' failure to understand—is concerned, this is so clearly brought out in 51b and 52 that we can, with a probability verging on certainty, attribute the ending of the pericope to the editorial work of the evangelist. The theme of the disciples' 'failure to understand', which has been in evidence shortly before in the miracle of feeding (6:37), runs like a red thread through the whole gospel (see 1:38; 4:13; 4:40; 7:12; 8:14-21; 8:32f.; 9:9; 9:19; 9:32 and 10:32), and reaches its climax in their lamentable failure in the passion story (14:26-31, 32, 42, 50f., 66-72)[3]—the ultimate consequence of their 'hardening'.

The fact that in the end it is the Roman centurion at the foot of the cross who, as the first *Gentile*, pays christological tribute to Jesus with the words: 'Truly this man was the Son of God' (15:39) is in harmony with the sequel in the 'longer ending', where even after Easter the *Jewish* disciples are reproached by the risen Christ for 'their unbelief and hardness of heart' (16:14).

It is hardly necessary to add here that a Jesus who chooses, of all people, disciples 'without understanding' to be the nucleus of his movement appears just as lacking in historical probability as an 'unbelieving' group of disciples, who have yet left hearth and home to follow their master wherever he may lead.

What we have here therefore is the product of editorial activity following the change, after A.D. 70, from Jewish Christianity to the Gentile Church.

(b) *Jesus as the new Jonah*

Verse 51a clearly raises different questions: 'And he got into the boat with them and the wind ceased'. At once these words remind us of the stilling of the storm (4:39), where, however, Jesus commands the wind and the waves: 'Peace! Be still!'—whereupon 'there was a great calm'. Here by contrast the 'ceasing' of the wind could easily be traced back to a 'divine passive', which might suggest an older strand of tradition. Here we see the pre-Marcan contours of a figure of Jesus who, while he acts with authority, is essentially earthly, and does not seem inclined to perform miracles, since he receives his authority solely from God.

The pericope as a whole has several textual similarities with the Jonah story. Both are concerned with a ship in distress; the crew, in Jonah, 'were afraid and cried out'; 'the men *rowed* hard to bring the ship back to land, but they *could not*, for the sea grew more and more tempestuous *against* them' (Jon. 1:13).

However, it seems that the miracle of deliverance is brought about in opposite ways in the two cases: in the case of Jonah the sea 'ceased from its raging' after Jonah was thrown *down* into it (Jon. 1:15), while in the case of Jesus it subsided after he got *up* to join the disciples in the boat (6:51).

Is Jesus here being depicted as a second Jonah, whose deeds surpass those of his forerunner? The contrast between Mark 6:51 and Jon. 1:13 does not seem sufficient to warrant this conclusion. However, when we remember that both were recognised as prophets in Israel (Mark 6:15); that it was only with great reluctance that both went to the Gentiles (Mark 7:24-30 and Jon. 1:1-3); and that nevertheless both finally achieved success among the Gentiles (Jon. 3:4-10, and Jesus in Mark's Gentile Church)—then it seems that a certain affinity of thought cannot entirely be ruled out.

This impression is strengthened by Matt. 12:39 ('the sign of the prophet Jonah'); Matt. 12:40 ('for as Jonah was three days and three nights in the belly of the whale, so will the Son of Man be . . .'); and Matt. 12:41 ('behold something greater than Jonah is here'); but especially by Luke 11:30 ('For as Jonah became a sign to the men of Nineveh, so will the Son of Man be to this generation').

It must also be added here that several Church Fathers, on the basis of Luke 11:29-30, stress the fact that the Gentiles paid attention to the message of Jonah, just as later Gentiles did to the apostolic gospel, while the Jews by contrast showed themselves to be disobedient—a fact which led to their punishment (see Justin *Dialogue* 107).

However that may be, the book of Jonah is regarded among believing Jews as the supreme expression of the unlimited nature of the love of God. As such it became the appointed reading from the prophets for the afternoon of the Day of Atonement—at a time, that is, when there was a danger that the fasting, penitent synagogue congregation might fall victim to complacency.

(c) *The end of the night as the end of the night of watching*

The nearness of the Passover festival (John 6:4), and the use, unique in Mark, of the word φυχαϰή in the sense of the night-watch, remind us of Isa. 21:12—a verse which early in the first century was already being used in the interpretation of the 'night of guarding' or 'night of watching' (Exod. 12:42), and was being understood messianically[4]: 'The Israelites said to Isaiah: "Our teacher, . . . how much of the night has passed?" He answered: "Wait for me, until I have enquired." When he had enquired, he came back to them. They said: "What does the watchman say? What does the watchman of the world (God) say?" He answered: "The watchman says: 'Morning comes, and also the night . . .'" (Isa. 21:12). They said to him: "And also the night?" He answered: "Not in the way you think; it is rather that the morning comes for the righteous and the night for the godless; the morning for Israel and the night for the nations of the world." They said: "When will the morning (of deliverance) come?" He answered: "When you wish; it is the will of God!" ' The ending of this passage from the Talmud seems significant, and it is in harmony with Jesus' call to repentance (Mark 1:15): 'They said: "What then hinders it (the coming of deliverance)?" He answered:

"Repentance. . . . Turn back (in repentance), come!" '5

The changing of the third and last night-watch (b. Ber. 3a) into the 'fourth watch' (6:48) in accordance with Roman reckoning is an example of the Hellenisation so common in the final editing of Mark.

The basic biblical thought that the time before the morning is the *kairos* for God's help (Isa. 17:14; Ps. 46:3); the longing for the ending of the night (of oppression and captivity), similar to the longing expressed in Isaiah's question to the 'watchman of the world'; and the danger which the night holds for opponents of Herodian power—all this may have led, here in 50b-51a, to a heartening experience of salvation, which, as it was related, acquired proleptic messianic dimensions.

3. THE ESSENTIAL MESSAGE OF THE PRE-MARCAN TRADITION: JESUS AS THE VICTIM OF
POLITICAL PERSECUTION

What can we now regard as the essential message of the pre-Marcan tradition?

The geographical indications seem to be helpful in the search for an answer. The conventional 'to the other side', which is one of Mark's favourite expressions,[6] and the subsequent 'to Bethsaida' in verse 45 are in tension with each other and in contradiction of the geographical facts, since this fishing village is situated to the north of the lake and on the eastern side of the mouth of the Jordan.

It is not surprising therefore that several manuscripts omit the words 'to the other side', and some of the Latin manuscripts replace 'to Bethsaida' with 'from Bethsaida'.[7]

The conclusion seems unavoidable that, so far as journeys by boat are concerned, we are dealing with fragments which do not seem to fit into any framework. The journey in 4:35 'across to the other side' begins in the evening and ends the next day (5:1ff.); the second journey, in 5:21, goes 'again to the other side', and seems to be forgotten until, in 6:32, the boat arrives in an unknown 'lonely place', near to which the feeding of the five thousand takes place. From there the boat travels, as has been said, in the direction of Bethsaida, only to arrive in broad daylight the next day at Gennesaret. The last time we hear of a boat journey is after the second multiplication of loaves in 8:10 and 8:13, after which Bethsaida is once more named as the place of arrival (8:22).

The only logical explanation for these anomalies lies in the supposition that in 4:35 and 6:45, as also in 8:13 and 8:22, it is a question of returning to a regular place for spending the night, in Bethsaida, to which, in view of its north-easterly situation, the western shore especially was the 'opposite side'. This agrees with all the topographical indications,[8] according to which the area on the Plain of Gennesaret, south-west of Capernaum, was the gathering-place for the large crowd which Jesus taught, fed and 'dismissed' (6:45).

But why did Jesus go regularly to the other shore in the evening? If the evangelist describes Jesus to us as time and again trying to get away from the crowds; if he had to 'withdraw' to the lake (3:7), and Herod Antipas began to be on the look-out for him (6:14-16); and finally if some of the Pharisees felt they had to warn him of a likely attempt at assassination by Herod (Luke 13:31ff.)—then it is obvious that the border-village of Bethsaida, which was outside Herod's territory, served him as a place of escape, from which he could continue to go out each day by boat to attend to the crowds on the other shore.

This may also explain why he had to 'make' his disciples go to Bethsaida without him (6:45), since they must obviously have known of the danger to which he was deliberately exposing himself if he spent the night over on the western shore. What he intended by it—whether he withdrew to the hills 'to pray' (6:46), or, as John says, to get away from the crowd who wanted to 'take him by force to make him king' (John 6:15)—we shall probably never know.

However that may be, it is highly probable that the Jesus with whom we have to do in the walking on the water is one who was being persecuted by the political authorities, one who had 'nowhere to lay his head' (Matt. 8:20; Luke 9:58). Perhaps this fact can help us towards a deeper understanding of Jesus.

Translated by G. W. S. Knowles

Notes

1. In Hebrew: Tischbi jetarez kuschiot we-baajot, according to Mal. 4:4-5.
2. See Paul Volz *Die Eschatologie der jüdischen Gemeinde* (Tübingen 1934) pp. 195, 236, 370.
3. Karl Kertelge *Die Wunder Jesu im Mk-Evangelium* (Munich 1970) pp. 146f.
4. See b. Sanh. 94a and Ex Rabba 18.
5. p. Taan I, 1.
6. πέραν occurs seven times in Mark. Six of the seven contexts must be regarded as editorial.
7. T. Snoy 'La Rédaction marcienne de la marche sur les eaux' EThL 44 (1968) p. 210.
8. G. Dalmann *Orte und Wege Jesu* (3rd ed.) pp. 139ff. Joachim Jeremias in ZNW 35 (1936) 180ff. sees Dalmanutha (Mark 8:10) as a misreading for *Magdala*.

Carlos Mesters

How the Bible is Interpreted in some Basic Christian Communities in Brazil

1. MARK 6:45-52 AS A FRAME OF REFERENCE

I WAS asked to take this text as the frame of reference for this article. As I have no specific information on how people in the communities interpret this particular text, I can only say something about how they see texts like this one, and describe the atmosphere in which they set about their process of interpretation.

The difficulties posed by this text will vary from one continent to another, and depend largely on the cultural context of the people reading it. The choice of this text, it would seem to me, was made in a situation in which the interpreter is dealing with a secularised people liable to raise considerable objections to such a text and unwilling to concede that anyone can walk on water or calm storms.

In Latin America, however, the interpreter is not speaking to a secularised or *non-believing* people, but to a deeply religious people, a believing people living in *non-human* conditions. An exploited people, often with the tacit support of the Church itself. In Latin America, the crisis of faith stems in the first place not from secularisation, but from the Machiavellian and diabolical aspect of oppression, fostered very largely by nations and persons who declare themselves Christian, and carried on in the name of a civilisation calling itself 'Western Christianity'. So, I thought: if the choice of text had been made on the basis of the situation in which people live in the communities of Latin America, it would have been something different. Who knows, it might even have been the one about the camel passing through the eye of the needle. . . .

Here too in Brazil, the difficulties posed by the text will vary. It depends who is reading it: someone from the wealthy classes; someone from the people who does not take any part in the life of the communities; a pastoral worker already more used to reflecting critically on social reality; or the people of the communities themselves.

2. HOW THE PEOPLE IN THE COMMUNITIES WOULD APPROACH THE TEXT

The people we are considering are generally poor—or rather, they are impoverished by the oppressive capitalist system: agricultural workers, labourers, dwellers in the shanty towns around the great cities, road-sweepers, refuse-collectors, domestic servants, washerwomen, etc. Faced with the Bible, these people do not (yet) show a secularised mentality. For them, the Bible is the Word of God transmitting its message to them *today*. This faith conditions the way they look at it and how they set about interpreting it.

They accept texts like this one in all naturalness and take up a stance not unlike that of the Fathers of the Church: they do not dwell on the text itself or the events it relates, but the text and the event soon become a basis and a starting-point for discovering a hidden meaning to do with their life today and the situation in which they live.

In discussing a text like this, the people are at the same time discussing their own lives, without making any great distinction of methodology or content. Biblical history, without ceasing to be history, becomes a sort of symbol or mirror of the present-day events they experience in their community. Life and Bible intertwine, each illuminating the other in the process.

Let us look at some examples that show the atmosphere in which the people of the communities read and interpret texts like this one:

(*a*) In a group of agricultural workers, meeting to discuss the Bible, in Goiás, the people were wondering who the angel could be who freed Peter from prison (Acts 12:1-17). Two versions were put forward. The first was José, who said: 'I was ill and told myself, "I am not going to let my illness stop me from going to the Bible group!" The illness was a sort of prison for me, keeping me in bed. But look here: the illness was also a way of helping me to see how many friends I had, since I never saw so many people in my house. There were also lots of people in St Peter's house. Then Fr Henrique came to visit me, and got into conversation with me. When he left, I began to feel better, so I got up and came to the meeting. So, if this was the time of the Bible, the people would have said: an angel of God freed him from his illness. And that's what it was!'

The second explanation was María's. She said: 'When Dom Pedro Casaldáliqa was arrested in his house, no-one knew. There was no communication. Seven armed policemen were guarding the house, not letting anyone in or out. Just like St Peter's prison in the Bible. But a little girl went in and they didn't take any notice of her. She took a letter from Dom Pedro out of his prison, went straight to the airport, posted it to the bishops who were meeting in Goiánia, and they roused themselves and succeeded in having Pedro set free. The little girl was the angel of God who made Pedro's prison doors burst open!'

(*b*) On the outskirts of Recife, a woman belonging to one of the communities was arrested and taken off in the police van. Frightened, she began to pray: 'Jesus, I'm afraid, so afraid I could betray my own brothers. But the gospel tells people not to be afraid when they're taken off to the tribunal. It also says not to worry about what you say to the police. So, help me to overcome this fear and speak for me!' The fear, however, got worse. She went into the police station with her legs trembling, terrified. But when they opened the door of the inspector's office, as she tells it: 'A strength came into my legs, the fear went away and such fine words came out of my mouth that I was amazed at myself. I thanked Jesus, for showing me that the word of the gospel is actually true!'

(*c*) A small community of agricultural workers in Linhares was read the text forbidding the eating of pig's meat. The people there asked: 'What is God trying to tell us today in this text?' They discussed the matter and came to the conclusion: 'Through this text, God is telling us that we, today, should eat pork!' Their reasoning went like this: 'God's first concern is with the life and health of his people. Now, pig's meat, when it's not well treated, can cause sickness and even death. So, in biblical times, God forbade the people to eat pork. But today, we know how to treat it; it's no longer a danger to our health. What's more, it's the only meat we've got to eat, so if we don't eat this meat, we're endangering the life and health of our children. So we should eat pork today, so as to be faithful to God!'

(d) At a meeting of communities held in João Pessoa, a working girl from São Paulo was commenting on the first reading at Mass, which spoke of the cry of the people (see Exod. 2:23-5). She said: 'The Bible says God heard the *cry* of the people. It does not say he heard the *prayers* of the people. I don't mean we shouldn't pray. I mean we should be like God. Lots of people work so that we can pray and join in communities. It is only later that we hear their cry. But I think our work should be directed, in the first place, to all the people who are suffering and weeping, and their cry should come to our ears first!'

(e) In a Recife slum, a lady said to a nun: 'Sister, today God has been to my house!' The nun asked how this was, and was told: 'I had no money to buy medicine for my little boy who is ill. Then, my neighbour was paid for a whole week's washing—100 cruzeiros. She gave it all to me so that I could buy the medicine. If that's not God, what is?'

These interpretations of the Bible and of life, so simple and yet so true, show something of how the people in the communities approach the matter of interpretation, how they see texts like Mark 6:45-52. Their attitude has three aspects that need analysing more closely, which might be summed up as: freedom, familiarity, fidelity.

3. STARTING POINTS FOR AN EXEGESIS BY THE PEOPLE

(a) Freedom of approach to the biblical text

The people of the communities show great freedom of approach to biblical texts. The basis of this freedom is not reasoning produced by a pastoral worker better educated than they, nor is it the result of a hard literary quest taught by some expert (nor could it be, since many of the people are illiterate; they cannot understand our reasonings, which are the fruit of an alien culture). In the examples given above, the freedom springs quite naturally from life experience. Other popular groups who lack this communitary and liberating experience of faith, tend to fix on the 'letter' of the text and fall into strict fundamentalism.

The Bible on its own is not capable of producing this freedom. On its own, it can only 'set our hearts on fire' (see Luke 24:32). For its meaning to be set free, a new experience of life is needed, an experience of resurrection (see Luke 24:28-30). Only then can eyes be opened (Luke 24:31), and the people begin to release the meaning of the Bible for their own lives.

This liberation from the prison of the letter on the basis of live experience is the first step in a long process which is just beginning. Sometimes, pastoral workers themselves fail to appreciate the importance of this first step. More rational in their thought-patterns, they try to free the people from the prison of the letter through questions concentrating on the historical aspect. 'Is that what really happened? Did the angel actually come into Peter's prison? Did Jesus really walk on the waters?' Such questions are important, but they are not the vital ones for initiating a process of interpretation.

It is far more important to pay attention to two things capable of generating this freedom in the people: (i) the value of the symbolic in life and events; (ii) the overall direction of the particular church to which the communities belong. As to the value of the symbolic: questions turning on historicity are not at the forefront of the concerns of people in the communities. The examples given show that they are neither fundamentalist nor historicist. If they would accept the text of Mark 6:45-52 without questioning it, this does not mean that they would take it literally. Their interpretation of the angel appearing in Peter's prison shows this clearly enough.

We who belong to a more rational culture discover the value of the symbolic after a long process of demythologization. For the people, the symbolic is a real dimension in their lives. They see the symbolic value of the events related in the text through a non-reflective process of intuition, since they see them with the same eyes as they see events in their own lives. But it should be remarked here that symbolic interpretation of events is not always the fruit of ingenuous, a-critical or pre-scientific consciousness. The people themselves are beginning to see that not everything can be explained in a symbolic fashion. At a meeting of ninety farm workers, many of them illiterate, they themselves raised the question: 'How is it that people know when to take a text literally and when not?' They then discussed this question in small groups, and came up with the following answer: 'A text should not be taken literally when: (i) it does not fit with the experience of people today; (ii) Jesus means it should be changed because of the commandment of love.'

The second factor that generates this freedom of approach to biblical texts is the overall direction of the particular church to which the communities belong. This brings us to the second aspect.

(b) Familiarity

The examples of popular interpretation given show a deep familiarity with the Bible. It is not the familiarity of someone who knows the Bible from end to end, but that of someone who feels at home with it. Before this renewal movement began, the Bible was always something that belonged to those who taught, commanded and paid, and was explained in such a way as to confirm them in the knowledge that enabled them to teach, the power that enabled them to command, and the possession of money that enabled them to pay. Now the Bible is beginning to belong on the side of those who are taught, ordered about and paid, and they are discovering that there is nothing in the Bible to confirm the others in their knowledge, power and money, which they use to control the lives of the impoverished people. They are discovering exactly the opposite of what was always taken to be a doctrine upheld by the Bible.

For some, the Bible is no longer a strange book belonging to 'the others', to 'the priest', 'the teacher' or 'the boss'. It is *their* book, and they read it with the same conviction as St Paul: 'This was written for us who are living in the last days!' This is a *new* way of seeing, and renews the content of what is seen. The Bible itself, particularly the Old Testament, will always be a complex book, with many difficult passages they cannot explain. But their interpretative approach to the Bible is something radically new. It comes not from our reasonings, but from a new way of experiencing the Church.

When the Church takes its pastoral line as one of commitment to the poor and consequent engagement in their struggle against injustice and oppression, then people's eyes are opened to see the Bible message in a new perspective. The people in communities struggling in concrete fashion for the liberation of the oppressed find in the Bible the history of a people like themselves and find God as 'a partner in the fight'. I once heard a lady in Ceará express this discovery like this: 'You don't need to go outside Ceará to understand the Bible!'

The exegete approaches the events of the Bible through his studies, which he carries out by means of his intelligence. But his body is not involved in the quest. The people approach with their feet. They follow the same road of suffering from which the Bible sprang. The harsh reality of their life today becomes the criterion for interpreting the ancient text and gives them a sort of natural affinity with which they see its real meaning in all its breadth.

In this way, a space is created in which the Bible can act, since 'Sacred Scripture should be read and interpreted in the same spirit in which it was written' (DV 12). 'And where the Spirit of the Lord is, there is freedom' (2 Cor. 3:17). It frees from the prison of the letter that kills, and frees the Bible itself, placing it on the side of the little ones who receive from the Father the gift of understanding the message (Matt. 11:25-6). In this way, we re-discover the importance of the old truth: the Bible is the book of the church (community), of the *'family* of God'. Without this wider context of a community engaged in a struggle for liberation, the people are lost in the Bible, which then acts like a microphone without loudspeakers. This leads to the third aspect.

(c) Fidelity

Jesus took the Bible out of the hands of the scribes and Pharisees and began to interpret it in a new way. His different interpretation led to conflicts. Today, by the fact of the Bible being once more in the hands of the people of the communities, it has 'changed places' and, in a sense changed classes. The fidelity with which the people are beginning to practise the Word is causing some disturbance and provoking conflicts. The main concern of the people is not to interpret the Bible, but to interpret their lives with the help of the Bible. They are trying to be faithful not to the meaning the text has in itself (its historical-literal meaning) but to the meaning for their own lives they discover in the text. Their growing interest in its literal meaning follows from their concern to validate or criticise the meaning they find in the Bible for their own lives and struggle.

So, for example, a group of nearly 100 farm labourers raised the following problems for discussion during a Bible-study meeting: '1. If the work the people do in the communities was thought out by the priests, is it communism or does it come from the Bible? 2. Does political education have anything to do with religion and the Bible? 3. Is our struggle to own our own land rooted in the Bible? 4. How is it that the harvest, as we can see, only brings profit to the rich and work to the poor? 5. One priest will read the Bible in a sense that the poor should rise up, and another in the sense that supports the rich: which of the two is right? 6. Should Christians take part in trade union struggles? 7. Is the Gospel only a question of prayer? 8. There is a catechism of slavery which the authorities taught the people before. Now there is a catechism of liberation which the people use. The authorities attack the people. How should they defend themselves? 9. In the celebration of the Word, should we only talk about God's things, or should we talk also about what we are doing to improve people's lives?' During the discussion, they themselves drew a distinction between *'the written Bible'* and *'the lived Bible'*. The lived Bible was their lives, in which they were trying to practise and embody the Word of God. And not only this: life itself is for them the place where God speaks.

In that meeting, the Bible achieved its objective, and disappeared like salt into food. All that was left was the food seasoned with the salt of the Word of God.

These three aspects: freedom, familiarity and fidelity, sum up the interpretative approach brought by the people of the communities to the Bible. It is just a beginning, a little seed just beginning to push through the soil, but full of promise for the future, since it is firmly rooted and authenticated in the past of the Church. These three qualities are not separated; they are organically fused into one, like coffee, milk and sugar in one cup: each affects the taste of the other two.

4. PROBLEMS THAT ARISE

Anything new brings problems and conflicts. There are communities in which hardly anyone can read. This is a challenge to creativity. The traditional methods of literary criticism are no use in these circumstances; so the people invent others: theatre, song, dramatisations, group discussions, etc. The general course followowed is one of free association of ideas; one concept leads to another. But as the novelty of first discovery wears off, there is an ever-increasing interest in the historical situation in which the people of the Bible lived. They want to know how society was divided into classes then, and what the material conditions of life were for the people to whom Jesus spoke. On this point, the 'materialist reading' of the Bible is proving of great service. Courses using this approach are multiplying. The most technical exegesis is starting to be questioned by this Church which has taken the Bible back into its own hands and wants an assessment made not from the point of view of the problem raised by exegetes, but from the standpoint of problems raised by the lives of the people themselves. In many places, there is a great thirst for the Word of God; this springs from a desire to deepen understanding of the struggle for liberation in the light of faith.

Despite all its faults and uncertainties, the interpretation of the Bible these people are making can make a great contribution to exegesis itself. The people's contribution is made not through spectacles, but through their eyes. The eyes of the people are recapturing the sure vision with which Christians should read and interpret the Bible. So this popular interpretation is a warning to the manufacturers of spectacles—the exegetes. Spectacles have to be made to suit eyes if vision is to be improved. When eyes have to be adapted to suit spectacles, vision is spoiled and the world grows dark.

Translated by Paul Burns

Allan Boesak

The Black Church and the Future in South Africa

1. BLACK THEOLOGY—BLACK UNDERSTANDING OF THE GOSPEL

WHITE POWER and white domination, oppression and the struggle for human liberation are still the overriding realities of the South African situation. These realities form the parameters within which the Black Church has to live and witness. It is of particular significance to note that the need to speak of a 'Black Church' is not confined to those in the traditional Black Churches alone. Blacks in the so-called multi-racial churches may no longer be excluded.

This is a happy development, because it means that in spite of so many things, the real meaning and significance of Black consciousness and Black theology has not completely by-passed the Christian Church.

(a) Black experience

Black theology teaches us that theology cannot be done in a void. It is always done within a particular situation. The situation of blackness in South Africa is the unavoidable context within which theological reflection of Black Christians takes place. We have come to realise that people are being influenced by their social and economic environment, and that their thinking is influenced by the social conditions in which they live. We recognise that Christians living in different situations will have different understandings of life, as well as vastly different understandings of the gospel and its demands for their lives. This is basically the answer to the question why for some people the gospel is an incomparable message of liberation, while others find in it justification for a system that exploits and oppresses.

So Black theology is a Black understanding of the gospel. This understanding is not confined to one group or denomination only, nor is it an automatic (universal revelation) to all Black people. It is rather the result of a painful and soul-searching struggle of Black Christians with God, and with the meaning of his Word for their lives today.

They have wrestled with a Black history—a history of suffering, degradation and humiliation through white racism. They have taken seriously the cry of so many Black people who through all the years have refused to believe that the gospel could be the narrow, racist ideology white Christians were yelling from Black pulpits and white theologians were giving respectability in their learned books. These Black Christians have come to the conclusion that the Church is where there is identification with those who suffer and are in need.

They were the people who refused to accept an anaemic gospel of subservience and dejection both in the blatant forms of a hundred years ago and in the subtle forms of the present. Somehow they always knew that the God of the Exodus and the Covenant, the God of Jesus Christ, was different.

(b) In search of a God of the oppressed

It was when they understood this that they walked out of the established, white-controlled churches to form their own. It was then that they rejected white theology and went in search for a God 'who walks with feet among you, who has hands to heal, a God who sees you, a God who loves and has compassion', to quote that great leader of one of the first African Independent churches, Isaiah Shembe.

These people knew that the gospel of Jesus Christ does not deny the struggle for Black humanity, and it was with this light from God's word that they went into the struggle, both within the Church and outside of it. And it is this understanding which today inspired so many Black Christians in their search for authentic humanity and a true Christian Church.

Out of this struggle, more than two centuries old, emerged the Black Church, a broad movement of Black Christians, consisting of Black solidarity transcending all barriers of denomination and ethnicity. It shares the same Black experience, the same understanding of suffering and oppression and the same common goal of liberation from all forms of oppression. It is a movement deeply imbued with the belief that the gospel of Jesus Christ is the total liberation of all people, and that the God and Father of Jesus Christ is the God of the oppressed.

(c) Blackness is a condition

But there is another point I have to make. We must remember that in situations like ours blackness (the state of oppression) is not only a colour, it is a condition. And it is within this perspective that the role of white Christians should be seen. Certainly I do not mean those whites who for so long have been leaders in the Black Churches. Nor do I mean those who happen to control those churches where Blacks are the majority. I speak of those white Christians who have understood their own guilt in the oppression of Black people as corporate responsibility, who have genuinely repented and have been genuinely converted. Those whites who have clearly committed themselves to the struggle for liberation and who, through their commitment, have taken upon themselves the condition of blackness in South Africa.

They are those who, in a real sense, 'bear the marks of Christ'. They are part of the Black Church, not as lords and masters, but as servants, not as 'liberals' but as brothers, for they have learned not so much to do for blacks, but to identify with what blacks are doing to secure their liberation.

This is the Black Church, and it is about this church that we will be concerned in this paper. Before we can begin to talk about the Black Church and the future, however, we will have to look at our present situation.

2. THE BLACK CHURCH IN THE PRESENT

What is the position of the Black Church in South Africa today? Let me suggest one or two things that should concern us.

(a) It is a Church uncertain of its identity

(i) The reality of white control

The Black Church in South Africa has not yet succeeded in attaining for itself an authentic identity. In many cases, white control is still a reality and that makes it difficult for the people to identify with the church. By 'white control' I do not only mean administrative control—although it is important who decides and really speaks for the Church—I am also thinking of the predominantly white image of the Black Church: in style, in witness, in commitment.

There is the question of the kind of structures blacks have inherited; structures geared to the needs of people who have no sensitivity whatsoever for the black situation. It is no wonder then, that the Black Church sometimes finds it so hard to respond meaningfully to black people in need of God's presence in their lives. A precondition for authentic identity of the Black Church is the ability to identify with the community which it serves.

It must identify with its past, its present and its future. It must become part of it, so that it may understand its joys, its sorrows, its aspirations. And the church must not be afraid to identify with the struggle of the people. For the struggle in South Africa is not merely political, it is also a moral one. The struggle is not merely *against* an oppressive political and exploitative economic system, *it is also a struggle for the authenticity* of the gospel of Jesus Christ. The struggle is as much against a political philosophy and practice, as it is against a pseudo-religious ideology. Apartheid and all that it stands for is not a system that places its fortunes on the political judgment of people. It demands, with idolatrous authority, a subservience and an obedience in all spheres of life, which a Christian can only give to God. (Of course, this in itself is not strange. Apartheid shares this with all totalitarian forms of government.)

(ii) The struggle for a Black humanity

To identify with the struggle is to realise that the struggle for liberation and the attainment of Black humanity is commensurate with the gospel of Jesus Christ. It does not mean that the Christian has to condone and justify everything in the course of the struggle. It does mean, however, that being *in* the struggle, he has the right to be the salt of the earth and the light of the world—*in the struggle*. Moreover, why should Christians, or even better: how can Christians stand aside and allow the struggle for our liberation to be monopolised by those who do not believe in the Lord Jesus Christ? And this whilst we know that the cry of the oppressed: 'How long, Lord?' will be heard by God?

No less a person than John Calvin reminded us of this when he wrote: '. . . Tyrants and their cruelty cannot be endured without great weariness and sorrow. . . . Hence these words: how long? how long? When anyone disturbs the whole world by his ambition and avarice, or everywhere commits plunders, or oppresses miserable nations, when he distresses the innocent, all cry out, how long? And this cry, proceeding as it does from the feeling of nature and the dictate of justice, is at length heard by the Lord . . . (the oppressed) know that this confusion of order and justice is not to be endured.

And this feeling, is it not implanted in us by the Lord? It is then the same as though God heard himself, when He heard the cries and groanings of those who cannot bear injustice.' (Commentary on Habakkuk, Ch. 2:6 Lect. CXI.)

Of course, John Calvin is right. So while acknowledging that the powers of the anti-Christ are at work in every situation, the Black Church knows full well that the refusal to participate in this struggle constitutes an act of disobedience to God. Also we know that where true human liberation takes place, it is because Christ is there.

It is within the heat of the struggle that Christians are today especially called to be the light of the world. *In the midst of* the struggle we are called to be the embodiment of God's ideal for his broken world. Christians must be there to represent God's possibilities for authentic Christians love, meaningful reconciliation and genuine peace.

(iii) *Not absorbed by the world*

In arguing thus, I cannot urge that the Black Church should be absorbed by the world, or that the struggle should dictate to the Church. It remains true that only a critical distinction from the world, i.e., holding onto the criteria of the gospel of its Lord, will enable the Church to make a meaningful contribution in keeping God's options open to people who in the midst of battle, through their tears, their fear or their anger oftentimes fail to recognise them. It is not a Christian struggle I am pleading for, it is for a Christian presence in the struggle that I plead.

This decision is not one that will one day face us—it is facing us now.

(b) *It is a Church facing a tremendous challenge*

The last decade has seen profound and rapid changes in the Black community in South Africa. These are not so much changes in tangible political structure as changes in political consciousness, which reached a peak in 1976.

Not all of the young who featured so prominently during that time have left the Church. Some of them have done so—in disappointment and disgust. Many of them, however, including their parents, are still in the Church, but with a highly sensitised political consciousness; with probing critical questions about the nature and the witness of the Church. These are young people with an experience far beyond their years, an experience born out of their active and personal engagement in the struggle for liberation and their God-given humanity. It is my contention that the Black Church does not yet know how to deal with this new, politically conscious generation.

This new political consciousness, together with the consciousness of Black humanity, have brought a new sense of responsibility in the Black community. This, plus their active involvement in the struggle, has taken away almost completely the traditional diffidence for the Church. Churchmen are no longer judged by their office and the authority it represents, but the office and the authority it claims are now measured by the active participation of these people in the struggle for liberation.

I daresay that although this worries us no end, we have yet to find an answer to these problems.

(c) *It is a Church dependent on an alien theology*

This I regard as most serious. At the basis of so many maladies in the Black Church, our inadequate life-style dependence on white sources, the very acceptance and rationalisation of the situation that makes us so dependent, lies our dependency on an alien theology.

(i) A theology of accommodation and acquiescence

For centuries the Black Church has been engaged in a struggle to speak truthfully. In this struggle, two theologies were fighting for supremacy in the Black Church. On the one hand there has been the theology we have inherited from Western Christianity: the theology of accommodation and acquiescence. An individualistic, other-worldly spirituality which had no interest in the realities of this world except to proclaim the existing order God ordained. This theology wanted blacks to accept slavery and, in modern times, their lowly position as second and third class citizens. Either through force of circumstances or through sheer hopelessness, blacks accepted this anaemic, heaven-oriented theology which today is still rampant in the Black Church.

(ii) A theology of refusal

On the other hand there was a theology of refusal. A theology which refused to accept that God was just another word for the status quo; a theology which understood that the God of the Bible is a God who takes sides with the oppressed and who calls people to participate in his struggle for liberation and justice in the world. This was a theology which understood God's love for his people and therefore uttered a clear No! against those who oppressed and dehumanised whether on slave farms, or native reserves, whether in the aseptic and air-conditioned temples of banks and boardrooms or within those dark and awesome buildings which house the prisons where so many brothers and sisters have lost their souls—and their lives.

This has been the theology of great Black leaders right through history: the theology of Denmak Vesey, Frederick Douglass, W. E. B. DuBois, Martin Luther King Jr., Nhemiah Tile, Mangena Mokone, Albert Luthuli—to name but a few. A theology expressed masterfully by Frederick Douglass:

'I love the religion of our blessed Saviour. I love that religion which comes from above, in the wisdom of God which is first pure, then peaceable, gentle . . . without partiality and without hypocrisy. . . . I love that religion which is based upon that glorious principle of love to God and love to men, which makes its followers do unto others as they themselves would be done by. . . . It is because I love this religion that I hate the slave-holding, woman-whipping, the mind-darkening, the soul-destroying religion that exists in America. . . . Loving the one I must hate the other; holding to one I must reject the other.'

This is the theology the Black Church must make its own if it is to survive, if it is to become truly Church. We must come to understand that this faith is not a 'new', a 'politicised' faith, but it is, rather, the age-old gospel, it is the message of the Torah and the Prophets. It is a message that unmasks the sinfulness of man, in personal life as well as in the social, political and economic structures he has built. It is a message that judges, but it also speaks of hope, of conversion and of redemption. It is a message for the whole of life. And it is our task to bring this message to our people in such a way that it makes sense in their situation.

3. THE BLACK CHURCH AND THE FUTURE

(a) The alternatives

So, after we have said all this, what about the future? Basically, there are two alternatives facing our country. One is to continue with the present trend of modernising and modifying white *baasskap* and eventually end up with a civil war; the other is to bring about radical and fundamental change which would inspire the search for a truly new society.

At the same time, the Black Church has two choices. It can develop a policy of *Realpolitik* and accommodation, urging the people to accept piecemeal concession, thereby making it easy for itself; or it can stand firm, challenging the forces of the status quo and accepting the risk that comes with it.

We should not deceive ourselves. This choice will not be easy. Now that all meaningful Black organisations have been banned, the Black Church has become more important than ever before as a vehicle of expression of the legitimate aspirations of the Black people. The Government knows this. That is why it is going to concentrate its repressive measures on the Church more and more. If the Black Church is going to be true to its Christ and its calling, I can see no way that the ultimate confrontation between the Church and this State is going to be avoided. The Government may also, however, try to persuade the Church that real changes are indeed taking place and that for the sake of peace, the Church should accept them. I think that we must expect a time when Government spokesmen will more and more employ a kind of Christian language, talking about love, peace and reconciliation, all for the purpose of undermining the watchfulness of the Church. Also many blacks, the so-called privileged under-privileged, might discover that they have more privileges still, and they may try to pressurise the Church. And here the Black Church is called to be wide awake to remember to take as its criterion not the privileges of those who already have more than others, but the justice done to 'the least of the brethern'. It must always remember that an evil system cannot be modified—it has to be eradicated.

Of course, the second choice is the harder one. It will leave no room for compromise. It is bound to bring confrontation, not only with the Government, but also with those Christians, white and black alike, who shout peace! where there is no peace. It will make the Church even more vulnerable. While the Government will accuse the Church of subversion, some Christians may shout charges of lovelessness and intransigence. But in the end the Church will have preserved its integrity. The Black Church, like Moses, is not called to negotiate with the Pharaoh—it is called simply to convey the Lord's command: Let my people go!

(b) Three tasks for the Black Church

May I suggest a few things the Black Church must do in order to equip itself for the future.

(i) First task

We must reaffirm our commitment to Jesus Christ. For the Black Church, Jesus Christ is Lord. He is Lord over all our life. This confession we must cling to at all cost. Our loyalty and obedience are to him alone. If the Black Church is to have any future at all, this is where we must be firm. Our allegiance is ultimately not to the laws of the State, nor to the laws of self-preservation, but to the commands of the living God. Our loyalty is to Christ, our criteria are the demands of his kingdom. We shall have to learn not to be dictated to by the demands of the status quo, however intimidating, nor by the demands of any ideology, however tempting. Our faith in Jesus Christ and the liberating power of his gospel must form the basis upon which we offer ourselves as humble servants in the world.

(ii) *Second task*

We shall have to learn to resist the temptation of what that great theologian of the resistance, Dietrich Bonhoeffer, has called 'cheap grace'. Love, peace, reconciliation, justice are evangelical realities the Black Church dare not ignore. But there is a danger in our South African Christianity today. Christians are sometimes so desperate for something 'good' to happen in this quagmire of political hopelessness that often they cannot distinguish between the substitute and the authentic thing. In such a situation, it is very tempting to see peace and reconciliation where there is none at all.

Oppression of black people in this country is 300 years old. In the course of these years, humiliation and degradation have left their mark on the souls of millions. Self-hatred and dejection have become the hereditory burden of countless generations. Many have died, many more will die. Distrust, suspicion, hatred have become part of our lives. Therefore, reconciliation is essential. But it will be costly.

In the process of reconciling God with the world, the confrontation with evil almost made Christ give up. But it was necessary. It was necessary to unmask man for what he really was. It was necessary to rip to shreds the flimsy garment of pseudo-innocence man has wrapped around himself to convince himself that he has no guilt. True reconciliation cannot happen without this confrontation. Reconciliation is not feeling good, it is coming to grips with evil. In order to reconcile, Christ had to die. We must not deceive ourselves. Reconciliation does not mean holding hands and singing.

'Black and white together', it means death and suffering, giving up one's life for the sake of the other. If white and black Christians fail to understand this, we will not be truly reconciled.

So it is with peace. One is not at peace with the God and the neighbour because one has succeeded in closing one's eyes to the realities of evil. Neither is peace the situation where terrorism of the defenceless is acceptable because it is done under the guise of the 'law'. For in South Africa, Adam Small's question remains pertinent: 'Which law? Man's law, God's law, devil's law?' Peace is not the absence of war or the uneasy quiet in the townships. Peace is the active presence of justice. It is the *shalom*, the well-being of all.

If our theology fails to make clear that Christian love is not a sentimental feeling but an act of justice, doing what is right, we have not understood the gospel rightly. We must not be afraid to say that in the South African situation Christian love between white and black must be translated into terms of political, social and economic justice if it is to be love. By doing this, we will help the Christian Church to accept the challenge of truthfulness and even though this process will be the much more painful one, it will be more authentic, and rewarding.

(iii) *Third task*

We must be prepared to meet the challenge the new situation will present. There will be the challenge to preach a relevant gospel to the Black community. For so many of our young people right across our land, the crucial question is whether the gospel is indeed the gospel of liberation, and not merely a white man's tool for the oppression of the poor. This is a challenge only the Black Church can meet.

There is also the challenge to find a way of participating meaningfully in the struggle. Words and statements will no longer suffice. With tragic inevitability, the violence inherent to the system of oppression in South Africa, breeds more violence and counter-violence. Also, as peaceful protest is being made increasingly impossible, the belief that violence is the only way out, is growing.

Now I know that the issue of violence is a touchy one, and this is not the place to discuss it. I want to say however, that the unbelievable hypocrisy of white Christians on this matter is appalling, and it will take all our resources to undo the damage done to Christian integrity on this point.

So while the debate is not yet closed, and while we may be faced with even more strenuous situations, we must in the meantime refuse to be idle. The Church must initiate and support meaningful *pressure on the system as a non-violent way* of bringing about change. The Church must initiate and support *programmes of civil disobedience* on a massive scale, and challenge especially white Christians on this issue. It no longer suffices to make statements condemning unjust laws and tomorrow to obey those same laws as if nothing has happened. The time has come for the Black Church to tell the Government and its people: We cannot in all good conscience obey your unjust laws because non-cooperation with evil is as much a moral obligation as is cooperation with good. So we will teach our people what it means to *obey God rather than man in South Africa*. A new study on the investment problem will not suffice. But direct and forceful action will show these companies how serious the Church really is about the plight of our people.

The Black Church must accept and understand that the rights of the oppressed are never given voluntarily by the oppressor. They must be *demanded* by the oppressed.

The time has come to realise that many of the things we talk about with pain year after year—economic injustice, exploitation, migrant labour—are maladies which are inherent to the economic system we adhere to, a system that our churches have all but sacralised. The Black Church must realise that if our economic system makes these evils necessary, then do not talk about the evils, change the system.

In any case it belongs to the task of the Black Church to search seriously for the kind of economics which would make possible the equitable distribution of the wealth of this land.

All of this does not preclude negotiation—but it does mean that we must be clear about both the preconditions and the framework within which negotiation is going to take place.

To do all of this in South Africa is to look for trouble. The repressive, intolerant nature of the present Government cannot allow this. And yet the Church has no other option. And whilst we do this we must prepare ourselves for even greater suffering. It is the Lord Himself who reminded us: 'A servant is not greater than his master . . .'. And for the Black Church the word of the Lord is especially true: 'He who wants to hold onto his life at all costs, shall lose it. But he who loses his life for my sake, shall gain it.'

If the Black Church can understand this, we will not have to fear the future.

So I pray that the Black Church in South Africa would, through the grace of God, be truly the Church of Christ:

> In the midst of struggle and in the heat of the battle—be a servant Church;
> In the midst of violence, oppression and hatred—be a prophetic Church;
> In the midst of hopelessness and pain—be a hopeful Church;
> In the midst of compromise—be a committed Church;
> In the midst of bondage and fear—be a liberated Church;
> In the midst of intimidation and silence—be a witnessing Church;
> In the midst of suffering and death—be a liberating Church;
> In the midst of failure and disappointment—be a believing Church;
> To God, the only God, who saves us through Jesus Christ our Lord, be the glory, majesty, authority and power, which he had before time began, now and forever!

Bernadette Brooten

Feminist Perspectives on New Testament Exegesis

WE ALL recognise that Paul's background as a Hellenistic Jew deeply influenced his theology and ethics. Yet if one dares to ask the question, 'Did Paul's maleness and the patriarchal society in which he lived deeply influence his theology and ethics?' one is likely to be greeted by scattered laughter, a brief silence and then a return to the 'more scholarly' questions.

Feminist scholars are now proposing that gender, like social class, religion, race, educational background and historical circumstances, is indeed a useful category of historical analysis and understanding. 'Gender' here does not just mean whether the author, the person written about or to or the interpreter is a man or a woman; it also implies the societal context. Concretely, an analysis based on gender must take into account that all of us live in patriarchal societies, that the New Testament was written in the context of patriarchy and that it has been passed down and interpreted by male-dominated institutions. Patriarchy (literally 'father-rule') implies that men control the government, the military, the bulk of the wealth and the institutions of religion and culture. The feminist movement holds that patriarchy is an unjust form of human organisation and works for the establishment of equal rights for women and men.

What does the patriarchal context of the New Testament imply for questions feminists might ask of it? The person looking to discover the history of early Christian women, their religious beliefs and experiences, their functions and their ethical values, will be disappointed at the meagreness of the sources. Those whose concern is male New Testament writers' attitudes towards women, more properly a topic of male psychology than of women's history, have considerable evidence to go on. In addition to such historical questions, feminists are also asking theological ones. Are New Testament concepts of God, redeemer, salvation, ethics, etc., adequate to an understanding of humanity which emphasises the equal dignity and equal rights of women and men? Should the New Testament canon be the normative base for feminist theological reflection? In the following I will try to indicate by the use of examples how feminist scholars are approaching these questions.

1. THE TRANSMISSION, TRANSLATION AND INTERPRETATION OF THE NEW TESTAMENT:
STUMBLING BLOCKS FOR WOMEN'S HISTORY?

Unlike the Dead Sea Scrolls or the Nag Hammadi Codices, the New Testament was not lost in antiquity to be rediscovered again only in our century. The New Testament has been copied and re-copied, translated and re-translated, and commented upon hundreds of times. Although more copyists may have been women than generally assumed,[1] nearly all editors, translators and commentators have been men working in a male-dominated Church and society, and one can occasionally detect an anti-woman bias in their work. Several examples will have to suffice here.

Acts 18:26 reads: 'He (Apollos) began to speak boldly in the synagogue; but when Priscilla and Aquila heard him, they took him and expounded to him the way of God more accurately.' A number of manuscripts[2] put Aquila first and Priscilla second. Apparently a reviser thought it unfitting that the wife be mentioned before the husband. In Col. 4:15 most text critics take 'Greet . . . Nympha and the church in her house', as original, but some manuscripts[3] have 'Greet . . . Nymphas and the church in his house'. Was some copyist troubled by a woman presiding over a house church?

In Rom. 16:7,[4] Paul greets two apostles. Virtually all modern translations give the second name (in the accusative IOUNIAN) as *Junias*, a masculine name, and the recent Greek editions accent the last syllable, i.e., as if masculine. All of the Church Fathers and, to my knowledge, all commentators on the text until Aegidius of Rome (1245-1316), took the name to be feminine, *Junia*. Further, the name *Junias* is not even attested in Greek and Latin inscriptions or literature, whereas *Junia* is a common Latin name. Literally all of the evidence speaks in favour of *Junia*. Why would editors and translators go against all of the evidence and prefer the masculine? The answer lies in the title 'apostle'. Since one imagined that a woman could not have been an apostle, then the woman called an apostle could not have been a woman.

2. THE NEW TESTAMENT ITSELF: THE EXTENT OF PATRIARCHAL INFLUENCE

These examples should encourage those in search of the history of early Christian women, for behind such distortions one may discover traces of women's history. It even seems that in certain early Christian communities, such as at Rome, women exercised leadership, enjoyed respect and were theologically influential.[5] Further, recent research on women as followers of Jesus and in the gospels has yielded a picture of women as more active and central to the evangelists' concerns than hitherto believed.[6] Women's theological and ethical reflections and their own account of their experiences, however, we do not have. Although the female authorship of one or more of the New Testament writings should not be excluded (assuming later ascription to a man), we have no positive evidence for this and should assume that most, if not all, of the New Testament was written by men. This would be in keeping with a tradition that women's ideas should not be heard by (1 Cor. 14:34) and that women should not teach men (1 Tim. 2:12). In other words, androcentrism is not just an issue of transmission and interpretation, but extends into the New Testament itself. This is evident not only in specific commands to women (Col. 3:18; Eph. 5:22-24.33; 1 Tim. 2:11-15; 1 Pet. 3:1-6), but also in theological reflection.

(a) Male dominance in the image of God

Heb. 12:5-10 is one example:

'And have you forgotten the exhortation which addresses you as sons?—

"My son, do not regard lightly the discipline of the Lord,
nor lose courage when you are
punished by him.

For the Lord disciplines him
  whom he loves
and chastises every son whom he receives" (Prov. 3:11f.).

It is for discipline that you have to endure. God is treating you as sons; for what son is there whom his father does not discipline? If you are left without discipline, in which all have participated, then you are illegitimate children and not sons. Besides this, we have had earthly fathers to discipline us and we respected them. Shall we not much more be subject to the Father of spirits and live? For they disciplined us for a short time at their pleasure, but he disciplines us for our good, that we may share his holiness.'

This text and its concept of God can only be fully understood within the context of patriarchy. The very distinction between 'sons' and 'bastards' only makes sense within patriarchal family structures, in which a male infant does not have value in and of himself, but only if he and the mother are attached to a legal father. Further, it is no accident that the author employs 'sons' rather than 'sons and daughters'; in the patriarchal family the daughter is less significant than the son, not worthy of mention. Finally, to grasp the meaning of God as 'Father' one must understand the structures of power within the patriarchal family. A comparison between the earthly and the divine is forced upon us by the text, which itself compares 'earthly fathers' to the 'Father of spirits'. God is, of course, superior to one's earthly father, but the text nevertheless appeals to a son's experience of being beaten by his father to convey a sense of who God is. The concept of God as Father here is based on the analogy of one's earthly father, whose authority as head of his family is in turn enhanced by the comparison. Thus, this Father God reinforces the structures of male dominance which provided the image of the Father God in the first place.

(b) The maleness of Christ

A discussion of feminist perspectives on the New Testament cannot pass over the central figure of the New Testament in silence. When the feminist philosopher Mary Daly proposed in her book *Beyond God the Father* (Boston 1973) that a male Christ is inadequate as a primary religious symbol for women,[7] liberal theologians opposing Daly's thesis were to be heard claiming that the maleness of Christ plays an insignificant role in Christianity. In 1976, however, the Vatican confirmed Daly's view in the *Declaration on the Question of the Admission of Women to the Ministerial Priesthood*,[8] which forbids priestly ordination to women, the main argument being that a woman could not represent the male Christ. The maleness of Christ is taken as a Christological category, a fact which 'cannot be disassociated from the economy of salvation' (*Declaration* 28). The declaration uses biblical texts, particularly those employing nuptial imagery, to support its view: 'That is why we can never ignore the fact that Christ is a man' (*Declaration* 30).

Are there New Testament texts in which the maleness of Christ plays a constitutive role? Although caution is demanded here, it does seem that in Eph. 5:22-33, Christ's maleness is essential to the symbolism and the ethical teaching:

'Wives, be subject to your husbands, as to the Lord. For the husband is the head of the wife as Christ is the head of the church, his body, and is himself its saviour. As the church is subject to Christ, so let wives also be subject in everything to their husbands. Husbands, love your wives, as Christ loved the church and gave himself up for her' (Eph. 5:22-25).

Significant for our question is the comparison between the husband and the Lord. A woman is to be subject to her husband as she is to her Lord, as if her husband, as 'lord', represented the 'Lord'. The husband, in loving his wife, is to love as the Lord loves (not as he loves the Lord); he thus represents the Lord in his marriage. As the Lord is the head of the church, he is the head of his wife. The maleness of Christ is, therefore, not incidental to this text, and the nuptial symbolism does not remain abstract, but is meant to affect women's daily life: they are to live in total subjection to their husbands. Their husbands are to love them, of course, but this only serves to reinforce the subjection.

Other feminists see other solutions to the problem of the maleness of Christ, such as that Jesus himself was a feminist[9] or that the revelation of God did not end with Jesus. This debate will certainly continue for years to come.

3. THE 'WOMAN QUESTION' WITHIN AND WITHOUT THE CANON

(a) Paul's ambiguity on the question of women

Feminists have discovered that looking beyond the boundaries of the New Testament canon can be very valuable. The development of two branches of the Pauline school can illustrate this. The genuine writings of Paul display an ambiguity on the question of women. On the one hand, Paul acknowledges and respects the work of women colleagues (Phoebe—Rom. 16:1f.; Prisca—Rom. 16:3f.; 1 Cor. 16:19; Mariam—Rom. 16:6; Junia—Rom. 16:7; Tryphaina, Tryphosa and Persis—Rom. 16:12; Euodia and Syntyche—Phil. 4:2; Apphia—Philem. 2) and he confirms that sexual distinctions are irrelevant in Christ (Gal. 3:28). On the other hand, he does not refrain from enforcing the social custom of the veil, which is a sign of submission, or from employing a hierarchy of God, Christ, man, woman as the theological rationale for this (1 Cor. 11:2-16). If 1 Cor. 14:34f. ('the women should keep silent in the churches . . .') is by Paul himself, and not by a later redactor, the tension would be even greater. This inconsistency is not logical, but feminists have come to recognise that very few men moving in the direction of acceptance of women as equals are consistent.

In time, however, consistency on the question of women did develop among Paul's followers. One branch of the Pauline school, represented by the *Pastoral Epistles* (1, 2 Tim; Tit.), argued, among other things, that woman should learn in silence and should not teach or have authority over a man (1 Tim. 2:11f.); woman was second in the order of creation (1 Tim. 2:13); Eve was deceived, but Adam was not (1 Tim. 2:14); women will be saved by childbearing (1 Tim. 2:15); women deacons (or wives of deacons?) should be serious, not slanderers, temperate and faithful in all things (1 Tim. 3:11); younger widows should remarry and not be enrolled as official widows of the community (1 Tim. 5:9, 11); women are especially susceptible to heresy (2 Tim. 3:6f.); older women should teach younger women to be submissive to their husbands (Tit. 2:3-5).

Let us contrast this picture with a writing of another branch of the Pauline school, *The Acts of Paul and Thecla*.[10] This work, which was not included in our canon,[11] but which was nevertheless translated into many languages and enjoyed wide popularity for centuries, is the story of a young woman who left family and fiancé to follow Paul. Twice sentenced to die, once for the crime of abandoning her fiancé and once for defending herself against rape, Thecla was saved by miraculous means. She baptised herself in the face of death, was rescued from death and later donned men's clothing and set out in search of Paul. When Thecla found Paul, he told her, 'Go and teach the word of God'. The work ends with, 'after enlightening many with the word of God, she slept a noble sleep'. 'Apostle' is one of Thecla's traditional titles.[12]

Concerning women, *The Acts of Paul and Thecla* are nearly diametrically opposed to the *Pastoral Epistles*.[13] Whereas the former offers women celibacy as an alternative to marriage, the *Pastorals* insist that women enter in patriarchal marriage. Whereas the women addressed by the *Pastorals* are told that salvation will come through childbearing, Thecla is neither mother nor bride. Whereas the *Pastorals* attempt to limit the office of widow to older women and insist that women learn in silence and not teach, *The Acts of Paul and Thecla* approvingly depict Thecla as evangelising.

These two schools of thought represent a solution to the ambiguity in Paul. *The Acts of Paul and Thecla* represent a continuation of Paul's preference for celibacy (1 Cor. 7:8f.), his collegiality with women and his view that gender distinctions are no longer relevant in Christ. The *Pastorals* represent a clear break with Paul's preference for celibacy, but are in continuity with his conservative views on social customs and women and with his rationale for these (1 Cor. 11:2-16). If 1 Cor. 14:34f. is by Paul, this would be a further point of contingency.

From the *Pastorals* and *The Acts of Paul and Thecla* we can see that there were at least two Pauline schools of thought on women. While *The Acts of Paul and Thecla* is not a model of feminist thinking, the figure of Thecla did offer women an alternative to patriarchal marriage, namely celibacy,[14] and she did serve as a model for women performing missionary activity. Tertullian attests that women in late second or early third century Carthage appealed to Thecla as a justification of their own right to baptise (*De bapt.* 17). Thecla was also a model for ascetic women in the fourth century.[15] This document was probably an especially effective instrument in the Church's mission to women.

I am not implying that the apocryphal writings are consistently more open towards women than the canonical ones, but rather only that ignoring the apocrypha would yield a distorted picture of women in early Christianity.

4. WOMEN AND THE CULTURAL CONTEXT OF THE NEW TESTAMENT

Much of the discussion concerning women in early Christianity centres on the significance of seeing it in its own cultural context, i.e., ancient patriarchy. This is a very important aspect, but feminists have learned to beware of monolithic depictions of Jewish or Graeco-Roman patriarchy created solely to make Christianity seem progressive.

For example, Jesus' forbidding of divorce (Mark 10:1-12 par.) is often taken as a sign of Jesus' desire to protect women from being arbitrarily divorced by their husbands, to whom was given the sole right of initiating divorce in Jewish law (Deut. 24:1-4; Mishnah tractate Gittin; Matt. 5:31f. par.). What is overlooked, however, is that Jewish legal thinking on divorce in that period was not uniform; some Jews recognised divorce initiated by women, while others did not. An ancient bill of divorcement issued by a woman has been found near the Dead Sea,[16] the Jerusalem Talmud makes reference to women's ability to divorce their husbands (Kethuboth 30b; Baba Bathra 16c), and the Jewish historian Josephus, who himself disputes women's right to initiate divorce, mentions two Jewish women who divorced their husbands (Jew. Ant. XV, 259f.; XX, 141-143). Mark 10:11 itself also presupposes women's right to initiate divorce (cf. 1 Cor. 7:10f.). Against this background, one can no longer simply declare that Jesus forbade divorce in order to protect women, a motivation which is also never mentioned in the gospels. While Jesus' forbidding of divorce would protect women from arbitrary dismissal by their husbands, it would also force women to remain married to husbands who abuse them.

The citation of this example is not meant to undermine the view that Jesus was open towards women, but rather to show that more detailed research on women in Judaism and in Graeco-Roman society is yielding a more differentiated background to the New

Testament. Hopefully we will soon be beyond the days when scholars allow themselves sweeping generalisations about the 'low' position of women in Graeco-Roman and especially Jewish society, all for the sake of contrast with the 'high' position of women in early Christianity.

5. MARK 6:45-52 AND PARALLELS

It would be an exaggeration to claim that any one method or approach can exhaustively explain every passage of the Bible, and the feminist approach is no exception. Feminist insights alone are insufficient for adequately interpreting the story of Jesus walking on the water, the theme passage of this issue. Feminists will simply notice the fact that the protagonist is a man and that the only other person mentioned by name is also a man (Peter—Matt. 14:28-31). Given the rather unusual nature of the event described, one might ask whether women would have been believed had it been they reporting the story (cf. how the women's report of the resurrection met with disbelief—Luke 24:10f.).

CONCLUSIONS

Even these few examples have shown that:

1. When one makes allowance for the androcentrism of certain copyists, editors, translators and interpreters of the New Testament, one can discover new evidence for the history of women in early Christianity, but we will never know as much about early Christian women as about early Christian men.

2. The influence of patriarchy on the New Testament extends even to the content of theological statements; there are some New Testament writers who consciously and actively try to maintain patriarchy by using biblical (O.T.) and theological arguments.

3. When one considers all canonical, as well as all extra-canonical documents of early Christianity, fragmentary remains of a highly variegated picture of theory and practice concerning women emerges.

4. Some scholars try to excuse the New Testament by pointing to its male dominated environment or to elevate it by painting a monolithically bleak picture of women in antiquity. Recent research, however, has yielded a more differentiated picture of women in the surrounding cultures.

5. A feminist approach cannot solve every problem of biblical interpretation, but it can shed light on many passages which have been dark for centuries.

Notes

1. Eusebius (*Eccles. Hist.* VI, 23, 2) says that Origen had girl copyists. Was this a women's profession at this time?

2. D it^{gig} syr cop^{sa} arm and others (i.e., the 'Western text'). For this and the following example, see B. M. Metzger *A Textual Commentary on the Greek New Testament* (New York 1971), *ad locc.*

3. D. K. and others.

4. See B. Brooten '"Junia . . . Outstanding among the Apostles" (Romans 16:7)' in *Women Priests. A Catholic Commentary on the Vatican Declaration* ed. L. and A. Swidler (New York 1977), 141-144.

5. See E. Schüssler Fiorenza 'Word, Spirit and Power: Women in Early Christian Communities' 'Female Leadership in the Jewish and Christian Traditions' in *Women of Spirit* ed. R. Reuther and E. McLaughlin (New York 1979) 29-70.

6. E.g. E. Moltmann-Wendel *Ein Eigener Mensch werden. Frauen um Jesus* (Gütersloh 1980).

7. Chap. 3 'Beyond Christolatry: A World Without Models' 69-97.

8. *A. Ap. Sedis* 69 (1977) 98-116.

9. L. Swidler 'Jesus was a Feminist' *The Catholic World* 212 (Jan. 1971) 171-183.

10. E. Hennecke and W. Schneemelcher *New Testament Apocrypha* II (Philadelphia 1965) pp. 353-364.

11. See Eusebius *Eccles. Hist.* III, 3, 5; 24, 3-7 (disputed, but not heretical); *Codex Claromontanus* catalogue (canonical): Hennecke and Schneemelcher I (Philadelphia 1963), 46.

12. See R. A. Lipsius and M. Bonnet *Acta Apostolorum Apocrypha* I (Leipzig 1891; photostatic reprint, 1959), 235; Psuedo-Chrysostom *Laudatio S. Protomartyris et Apostolae Theclae*: Migne, *Patr. Gr.* 50, 745-748; Anonymous *The Life and Miracles of Saint Thecla* ed. G. Dagron (Brussels 1978) *passim*.

13. See D. MacDonald 'Virgins, widows, and Paul in Second Century Asia Minor': *Society of Biblical Literature* (1979) *Seminar Papers* I (Missoula, MT., 1979) 169-184.

14. On virginity as freedom from submission to a husband, see Cyprian *De habitu virg.* 22: *Corp. Script. Eccl. Lat.* 3, 1, p. 203; Leander of Seville *De institut. virg.*, preface: *Migne, Patr. Lat.* 72, 880A.

15. See Gregory of Nyssa *Vita Macrinae* 2: *Sources Chrét.* 178 p. 146; Ambrose *De virg.* 2, 3: *Migne, Patr. Lat.* 16, 223f.

16. P. Benoit *et al Discoveries in the Judean Desert* II (Oxford 1961) p. 108.

PART III

Josef Blank

The Authority of
the Church in the
Interpretation of Scripture

1. THE RECOGNITION OF EXEGESIS BY THE MAGISTERIUM

SINCE THE appearance of *Divino Afflante Spiritu*, Pius XII's encyclical on the furtherance of modern biblical studies during the Second World War (1943), hardly any theological discipline has received the same kind of generous encouragement and promotion from the official Church accorded to modern exegesis. In fact this encyclical removed a taboo that until then had disabled exegesis as a consequence of the anti-Modernist trauma. Henceforth the exegete was enjoined to 'try with the utmost care, and without neglecting any data provided by recent research, to establish the manner of expression and situation of life of the biblical writer, in what period he lived, what oral and written sources he used, and what literary mode he adopted. In this way [the exegete] will more adequately recognise who the biblical writer was and what his intention might have been. No one should forget that the most important rule for the exegete is to determine precisely what the writer intended to say.'[1] Hence the establishment of the literal sense of Scripture as well as the study of particular literary modes was acknowledged to be the most important task of exegesis.

The *Dogmatic Constitution on Divine Revelation* of the Second Vatican Council[2] adopted these recommendations and promoted them enthusiastically. The third chapter of the Constitution on Revelation contains a summary hermeneutics of the interpretation of Scripture which allows exegesis the freedom of movement necessary for scholarly activity, without imposing any restriction on it. The exegete, says the Constitution, must be aware of the literary modes used, for the truth is always conveyed and expressed in texts which are variously historical, prophetic or poetic, or composed in accordance with the norms of other forms of discourse.[3] Here—and this seems noteworthy—it is accepted as self-evident that the Bible (O.T. and N.T.) contains not only historical or prophetic texts but 'poetic' writings; and therefore that divine truth can also appear in the form of literature, myth or legend.

2. THE CONSEQUENCES

(a) Recognition of the precedence of the question of literary mode

Though it may perhaps seem superfluous, one has repeatedly to insist that the question of the literary mode or 'genre' of a biblical text is of primary importance for its understanding; that the decision to accord it to this or that mode is of crucial importance for the discernment of the truth of a particular text.[4] In any case it is inappropriate to approach biblical texts with a one-dimensional ontological or dogmatic notion of truth and to interpret them accordingly, because such a procedure sometimes (or, rather, usually and frequently) obscures the expressive intention of those texts.

Hence, to cite an appropriate example, the so-called 'infancy narratives' of Matthew and Luke (Matt. 1-2; Luke 1-2) must be classified according to literary mode before attempting any dogmatic statement on the 'virgin birth'. Moreover the 'infancy narrative' category is to be found not only in the Old Testament but in comparable non-biblical literature of the ancient world; I need cite only the 'parallel biographies' of Plutarch or the 'histories' of Herodotus, which prove the point on close examination. One soon learns that many famous men, once they had achieved something in history, were also endowed with just as significant a childhood—one marked by extraordinary events, even when historically speaking little or nothing was known of their infancy.

(b) Recognition of the historico-critical method

Even poetic texts or legends can contain truth and transmit it, according to the Constitution on Revelation, and once this is fundamentally conceded then exegetes too are entitled to use such insights, and not merely in the Old Testament (where obviously there is greater readiness to do so) but in the New Testament, wherever the text requires such an approach. A similar point may be made in regard to the historical approach to biblical texts. Hence, according to the 'Instruction on the historical truth of the Gospels', the exegete has to take into account 'the three phases of the handing-on process': ((i) the historical Jesus; (ii) the tradition of the community; and (iii) the editorial work of the evangelists) 'by means of which the teaching and life of Jesus have been handed down to us'.[5] This is a clear acknowledgment of the method of 'historico-critical inquiry into the historical Jesus', which fundamentally excludes any naive dogmatic and fundamentalist understanding of the Bible. At the same time there is recognition of the already classical distinction between the 'Jesus of history and the Christ of faith'.

In fact Catholic exegesis can rely on the magisterium's official recognition of modern historico-critical methods in a way inconceivable fifty years ago. As Rudolf Schnackenburg says: 'In the present situation, which is characterised by the rapid development of theology and of the Church after the Second Vatican Council, exegetes enjoy true freedom to investigate with all reasonable means and methods the conditions in which the books of the Bible originated, the expressive intention of the biblical authors and the meaning content of biblical writings in the historical context of their origins, and in addition to place them in a context of present-day problems. The relation of exegesis to the "authoritative interpretation of the Church" has to be reconsidered. The last Council showed in a most stimulating way that theologians are accorded significant weight in the formation of the judgment of the magisterium; that this judgment is not uniform (compromises and majority decisions!); and that there is a reciprocal relationship between scholarly theology and the exercise of authoritative teaching, so that a constant exchange of opinions and dialogue is required'.[6]

(c) Exegesis as the soul of theology

It only remains to remark that in the most varied decrees of the Second Vatican Council, the significance for theology as a whole of Scripture, and of its study and reading, is firmly stressed. 'Sacred theology relies on the written word of God, together with sacred tradition, as on a lasting foundation.'[7] Students of theology and candidates for the priesthood 'should be especially encouraged . . . to study Holy Scripture, which must be the soul of theology as a whole'.[8]

All this sounds marvellous, but what is it like in reality? The reaction of an exegete reading the foregoing passages is somewhat mixed. Of course it is right and proper that modern exegesis should enable the Bible to speak with the aid of all those methods which are available nowadays. To be sure it is also the positive intention of exegesis to serve theology, faith and proclamation. But here the difficulties begin.

3. THE DIFFICULTIES

(a) The material problem

Let me begin with the most immediate problem: that is, the normal form of proclamation and the interpretation of Scripture in the liturgy with all its prescribed readings. This form of proclamation in particular depends essentially on the aid of exegesis. For it is not enough to offer churchgoers a greater selection of biblical texts which they really do not understand. The normal Sunday-churchgoing Christian is taxed quite enough by three liturgical readings.

Let me give an example. If, say, we consider the readings for the sixth Sunday of Easter (11 May 1980), we have the following: first reading: Acts 15:1-2, 22-9; second reading: Rev. 21:10-4, 22-3; third, gospel: John 14:23-9. No responsible exegete could be satisfied with this selection of different kinds of texts (the council of the apostles; the heavenly Jerusalem of the Apocalypse; a Paraclete text from the Gospel of St John). There is no obvious internal relation between them. In addition there is the silence of the company in Acts 15, which in itself is a significantly expressive passage on an important theme, yet is quite mangled in the version offered. What the exegete cannot do is still less to be expected of the normal lay-person.

The new order of readings, which is intended to allow the Bible expression in the liturgy and to make it more familiar, all too often leaves the laity in silence. It certainly needs basic revision. One cannot escape the impression here of a magical understanding of the Bible in the background, of an automatically-effective 'Word of God', together with a liturgical form of allegory full of esoteric refinements that no outsider can ultimately penetrate. What is to be done? Probably what intelligent preachers have done for ages: which is usually to restrict themselves to a single reading but to deal with it thoroughly. The sensible course is to select a text and a topic, to concentrate one's preaching on it, and to disregard the others as inessential and profitless. On this basis, too, it is possible to use exegesis sensibly.

Since the allegorical method is now out-of-date and so involved as to alienate the modern congregation, a fruitful interpretation of biblical texts is possible only on the premiss that they are understood in the sense permitted by modern biblical hermeneutics.

(b) The hermeneutical problem

To be sure, the normal form of proclamation in a parish is also the decisive test-case and starting-point of *the hermeneutical problem*. The saying of the liturgy in the vernacular together with biblical readings has already made the hermeneutical problem a central question for the ordinary parish. It was obvious in times past that most people did not understand most of the Latin texts they listened to. But nowadays, with even the best translations, we are faced with the problem of direct access to the texts and therefore a clear apprehension of their alien nature, cultural and ideological difference, and therefore the urgent necessity of an explanation. This has to be an explanation which, if it is not to peter out in superficial uplift, is possible only on the basis of an intensive examination of a specific text. Here precisely, it is obvious that standard dogmatic theology, even in the 'rule-of-faith' form, is no longer of any real use, because it still depends on a pre-critical form of exegesis which takes into account neither modern exegetical methodology nor the change of historical consciousness.

(c) The problem of the 'success' of the historico-critical method of exegesis

I do not have to prove that the abovementioned problems of ordinary Church life are a major reason for many hotly-disputed questions of the moment: their common denominator is the hermeneutical problem, necessary interpretation and all the associated worries. At this point I must remark that the official Roman theology has gravely underestimated both the premises and the consequences of historico-critical methodology. It has been thought possible to allow exegesis room for action as long as it stays within the purely historical horizon of its sphere of operations and confirms or, best of all, never touches on dogma. But as soon as biblical theology becomes really up-to-date, and raises theological questions of our time (which it has to do in regard to the liturgy!), and when prophetic and charismatic or even merely historical criticism of the Church, theology and the history of dogma and so on, is brought into play on a scriptural basis, it suddenly no longer seems to be made so welcome as the 'soul of theology'. Then we are faced with sharp conflicts and long-term problems. Behind it all we have to deal with the problem that the historico-critical method is never a neutral, value-free instrument of research which can be used in a purely technical way in the service of a system constructed along quite different lines, but that it represents *another way of thinking* and *another way of seeing*, which conceives theological thinking as a whole and therefore its detailed applications *in a different way*. Here we are concerned with changes in consciousness which to some extent are still not appropriately taken into consideration, which have to be applied in the long run, and which cannot simply be controlled or blocked at will.

4. AUTHORITY OF THE CHURCH—AUTHORITY OF SCRIPTURE

If the 'authority of the Church' is to be invoked appropriately in this context, then that is possible only if it submits to modern conditions of discussion and understanding; otherwise it will stay apart from what is really going on and miss the essentials, as is shown by the earlier decisions of the Biblical Commission. In other words, here we are faced with the fact that the *'authority of the Church' itself is dependent on the same Scripture as exegesis*, and that both have to reveal the premises of their understanding and cooperate if they are ever to do justice to one another. This is all the more true in that, if we are to believe the official pronouncements of the magisterium on exegesis, that same magisterium has sanctioned and accepted modern methods and approaches to understanding. Hence we may presume that the same magisterium will remain loyal to its own pronouncements and can be interrogated in that regard. Moreover it has been shown that the interpretation of Scripture is a very finely-nuanced process which takes place in many different areas and situations, not only in scholarly exegesis. It occurs wherever the Bible is applied with practical reference to actual human situations—something which is obviously quite different in South America and in Rome. Ecclesiastical authority is hardly something which can be so unambiguously determined in regard to the interpretation of Scripture as is possible in the areas of dogmatic theology and canon law; in the case of exegesis it is more obviously apparent that biblical truth has its own autonomous authority, as against, as it were, the Church as a whole. If we look at things in this light, the Bible and exegesis in the Church may be viewed as entities in their own right, with their own life and effects, which are not so easily manipulated by the magisterium. Instinctively one thinks of the parable of the sower and the seed with its varying fate; an image that offers grounds for nothing but optimism.

Translated by John Cumming

Notes

An especially important reference is *Die Exegese in der Theologie*, being *Theol. Quartalschrift Tübingen* 159 No. 1 (1979), containing J. Blank, 'Exegese als theologische Basiswissenschaft' 2-23, and the corresponding articles.

1. Pius XII, encyclical *Divino Afflante Spiritu* on the modernisation of biblical studies, 30 September 1943. Latin-German edition (Freiburg im Breisgau 1947) p. 41.

2. LThK *Das Zweite Vatikanische Konzil*, 3 vols. (Freiburg im Breisgau 1966-8) II pp. 497-583.

3. *Constitution on Revelation*, ch. III, art. 12, LThK II, p. 53; see Blank, 'Exegese . . .' the article cited at the beginning of the notes, at p. 8.

4. See K. Koch *Was ist Formgeschichte?* (Neukirchen [1]1964); G. Lohfink *Jetzt verstehe ich die Bibel. Ein Sachbuch sur Formkritik* (Stuttgart 1973).

5. *Instructio de Historica Evangeliorum Veritate*, 20 April 1964, ed. J. A. Fitzmeyer, SBS 1 (Stuttgart [3]1966), VI, p. 2; see also *ibid.*, pp. 21ff.

6. R. Schnackenburg 'Der Weg der katholischen Exegese', in *id. Schriften zum Neuen Testament. Exegese in Fortschritt und Wandel* (Munich 1971) pp. 15-33, epilogue p. 32.

7. *Constitution on Revelation*, ch. VI, art. 24; see also art. 22-5.

8. *Decree on Priestly Formation*, LThK, II, pp. 309-355, art. 16, p. 343.

James Barr

The Fundamentalist Understanding of Scripture

FUNDAMENTALISM IS a tradition of Protestant Christianity, identified by its strong emphasis on the absolute authority of Scripture, understood to be inspired and infallible. Its roots lie in the confessional orthodoxy of the eighteenth century; but the closer affinity of most modern fundamentalism is with the evangelical 'revivals' of the nineteenth and twentieth centuries. Revivalism, with its emphasis on sin, personal conversion, experience of the Holy Spirit, the 'Second Coming' and final judgment, is its normal religious context and pattern. Though similar tendencies are found elsewhere, the total complex of fundamentalism is a purely Protestant phenomenon. Various terms, such as 'conservative evangelical', 'Bible-believing', 'high doctrine of Scripture' and the like, are commonly euphemisms for fundamentalism or for a position strongly influenced by its ideology.

Fundamentalism is a coalition between various groups, the common ground between them all being the conservative or infallibilist view of Scripture. Traditional orthodoxy, though still affirmed, has been transformed in many ways: elements formerly essential (e.g., predestination in Calvinism) became optional. Fundamentalism thus has a certain 'ecumenical' dimension, relegating to peripheral status some traditional dogmatic controversies, so long as biblical infallibility is preserved. But it is bitterly polemical both towards Catholic doctrine, which it supposes to put the Church in the place of Scripture, and towards modern critical theology and biblical criticism, which it labels as 'modernist' or 'liberal' and supposes to have put 'reason' or intellectual fashions in the place of Scripture. Much fundamentalist rhetoric is not really exposition of Scripture but inculcation of this basic ideological picture of the theological scene.

1. THE DOGMATIC POSITION

For fundamentalists, Scripture comes from God and is inspired in all its parts. It provides the basis for preaching and for practical impact upon personal life. The typical assertion of the evangelist is 'The Bible says' (not so often 'The Bible means'). That same inspiration of Scripture, which makes it so final and complete as a doctrinal and practical authority, means also that it is reliable in historical regards. To separate different sources within a book, to suggest that it comes from a writer of a later time, to explain it as originating out of human conflicts in Israel or in the Church, is thus not only to cast doubt on its historical accuracy but to undermine its spiritual authority. Fundamentalists thus believe that all claims about the authority and saving work of Christ are absolutely dependent on the reliability of Scripture and that the content of Christian faith will be evacuated if any deviation from this view of Scripture is allowed. The idea that Scripture is derived *from* the Church and is a reflection of, rather than the ground for, the authority and saving work of Christ receives little consideration among them. From the fact that the Bible is—necessarily—the starting point in the sense of the basic written source, the fundamentalist concludes also that the theological verities are actually *dependent* on the status of Scripture.

It is easy to show that this view is not derived from Scripture itself but is an imposition of Protestant tradition upon it. The men of the Bible themselves did not live by Scripture in the way that fundamentalists require. St Paul believed in the risen Christ without having seen a written gospel. Jesus never commanded or sanctioned the production of a written New Testament. The famous text (2 Tim. 3:16), beloved of fundamentalists, which mentions inspiration says nothing about historical accuracy, makes no suggestion that the inspired Scripture is the central criterion of faith, and commends it on the humble practical ground that it is 'profitable' for training in righteousness. These facts however are not perceived by fundamentalists. They are convinced that their own view of Scripture is the view which Scripture itself insists upon. And of course texts indicating the importance of Scripture can rightly be quoted, e.g., the authoritative role of the Old Testament for the men of the New.

Nevertheless, even making such allowances, it remains that the fundamentalist view of Scripture is a *general* principle and a view 'from above'. It does not start from the detailed factual realities of the Bible: it begins as *a dogmatic position* which was formed in the past and is *imposed upon Scripture*; the supposed scriptural evidences for it are valid only when this dogmatic position is already accepted. The original reasons for this dogmatic position have now altered and the entire context has changed; but the same view continues to be applied to Scripture. Thus the fundamentalist view of Scripture is no longer (if it ever was) a means to enable Scripture to express itself freely; rather, it is a means by which Scripture can be made to serve as the essential expression of the evangelical tradition in religion.

2. PRINCIPLES

(a) Revivalist conversion

The actual content of fundamentalist interpretation follows the contours of evangelical religion. Passages about *forgiveness* and justification are referred to the revivalist conversion, calls to follow the Master are interpreted as appeals to 'decide for Christ'; references to hell and damnation are exploited as means to induce the uncertain to seek salvation; eschatological pictures are built into the traditional evangelical picture of the 'Second Coming'. Passages which might lead towards a different theology or churchmanship are neglected or taken as peripheral.

(b) To confute the rationalism

Interpretation is *strongly harmonising* in character. The differences between two strands of the Pentateuch, or between Acts and the Pauline letters, are not taken to mean a real discrepancy either in historical fact or in theological outlook. The harmonisation, however, being structured upon the evangelical religious tradition, gives a distinct shape to the whole, that is, one of correspondence with the fundamentalist form of religion.

In spite of its naive and simplistic style, fundamentalist reading has a distinct philosophical colour, which is markedly rationalistic. The rationalist heritage corresponds with the fact that fundamentalism is at its strongest in the lands of Anglo-Saxon culture. The eighteenth-century debates, in which apologists used reason *to confute the arguments of unbelieving rationalists*, live on in fundamentalism. Truth is indicative: biblical sentences are assertions which state fact, which correspond with reality. To read them otherwise is necessarily to deny that reality. The Kantian heritage, suggesting that meaning is reached through a framework that we apply to the world, is correspondingly neglected or rejected: for it would suggest, rightly, that the 'evidence' perceived by fundamentalists for their views is there only for one reason—that they are fundamentalists from the beginning anyway.

(c) To safeguard the truthfulness of Scripture

Fundamentalist interpretation, however, is not always literal. The principle that the Bible must be true overrides the preference for the literal. Where modern science makes difficulties for a literal understanding, a figurative or non-literal interpretation is readily adopted in order *to safeguard the truthfulness of Scripture*. With this proviso, however, fundamentalist interpretation remains substantially literal at many key points, and thus it lays substantial factual reality upon the referents or events indicated in miracle stories, the virgin birth narrative, the sequence of eschatological events, heaven and hell. All these are real entities, correctly stated by the biblical text.

This view of the truth-character of Scripture is often well expressed with the favourite term '*claim*'. Fundamentalists think that the Bible 'claims' to be inspired and accurate, just as they think that Jesus 'claimed' to be God. This phraseology makes the Bible appear as a document requiring *assent*, the only alternative being denial. In spite of the powerful witness of the gospels that Jesus strongly *avoided* 'claiming' to be God or Son of God, this 'claim' is vehemently insisted on, and is supposed to be *the reason* why we speak of the divinity of Christ. The emphasis in Christology is on the divinity of Christ: not that his humanity is denied, but it is taken as something obvious, which even non-believers accept, while his divinity is the element that has to be positively believed, and that on the ground of Scripture.

(d) An example

In actual exegesis the outworking of these principles is often jejune and uninspiring, thin in theological content. Our passage on the walking on the water (Mark 6:45-52 par) well illustrates this. A standard commentary of the sort accepted by fundamentalists (*The New Bible Commentary Revised*, 3rd edition, London, 1973, pp. 835, 865-6, 942) displays an insistence that the miraculous incident really occurred. There is absolutely no difficulty in taking the walking on the water as a literal (physical) fact, since, if Jesus was Incarnate Deity, there was no problem. But, this being so, the significance of the whole is largely exhausted. We learn of his 'power over the natural order' (p. 835) and that 'fear is banished by the realisation of the presence of Jesus (p. 942). Curiously, space is given to refuting the rationalistic explanation that Jesus was really walking not on the sea but on the shore. Apart from the insistence that the incident really occurred as described, little specific theological content emerges.

3. TYPICAL CONSEQUENCES

(a) Assertory character

This is typical of fundamentalist interpretation: the actuality of referents and events is *much emphasised*, but *significance* is *thinly* perceived. The fact that the Bible is right is indeed itself its essential meaning. The inner dynamics of the Bible, its growth from stage to stage, the conflicts between its theologies, its dependence on earlier tradition, the entire antecedence of the faith and the Church to Scripture, are little reckoned with. The poetic and figurative character of language are not denied, but except in marginal cases they are not permitted to *replace* the essential *assertory* character ascribed to biblical language.

(b) Scriptural infallibility

Scriptural infallibility, being a *general* relation, operates as a rational nexus: once it is known as a general principle that all Scripture is true and fully true, it then rationally follows that all its detailed statements are true. Conversely, if any point in Scripture is doubted, that makes another doubtful, and that overturns another, and in the end no assurance about anything will remain. This rationalist argumentation minimises the possibility of faith wrestling with God through a particular scripture, without a universal assurance about *all* of Scripture. Instead of the content of each passage being part of the problem of faith in God, *the truth of Scripture is decided generally and in advance*. This rational nexus explains why the doctrine of scriptural infallibility is normally pressed to extremes, and also why historical apologetic methods, seeking to prove the correctness of Scripture at each point in order to maintain the truth of the whole, are so prominent.

(c) Influence of ideological leaders

According to fundamentalist doctrine, the relation between Scripture and Church is plain: the duty of the Church is to submit itself to Scripture. Compared with this imperative, other questions about form and organisation of the Church are of secondary importance. In fact however it does not work out so simply. Nothing is more striking in fundamentalism than the prominence of *human authority*. The ideological leaders or *gurus* of fundamentalism have much greater influence in their constituency than have bishops, theologians or biblical scholars in non-fundamentalist Christianity. Their power to declare and mould the meaning of Scripture is tremendous. But they retain this power only so long as they continue to profess devotion to biblical infallibility and allegiance to the partisan evangelical cause. Similarly, the great evangelist, like Billy Graham, functions as a living manifestation of the evangelical ideal and confirms that tradition in the eyes of its believers: that is what he is there for. Again, conservative scholarship functions to provide fundamentalists with the assurance of intellectual respectability which they so greatly crave. In these ways fundamentalism, in spite of its profession of submission to Scripture, actually uses that profession to maintain the human authority of the group consciousness and its leaders.

(d) Personal experience

Fundamentalism also has a strong stress on *personal experience* and guidance: there is a sympathy for direct communication from God, and here again fundamentalism is

F

less exclusively biblical than it seems to be. Fundamentalists like a person to say that God actually spoke to him and told him or led him to do this or that. Charismatic experience of the Holy Spirit, and faith healing, are similar. Though often associated with fundamentalism, these open up another perspective: they mean that there is a communication or experience that comes straight from God: this is a new channel of communication, alongside Scripture. Of course it is thought that Scripture validates these experiences: but Scripture is then performing a confirmatory role. It confirms that such experiences are valid, but this does not alter the fact that these experiences, rather than Scripture itself, become the actual and living main channel of communication and relation with God. In all these aspects fundamentalist spirituality, paradoxically, comes closer to a 'liberal' than to a strictly scripturally-controlled pattern.

(e) Millenarianism

Another aspect of fundamentalism is its connection with *millenarianism*. Some fundamentalists play down this connection and certainly not all are millenarians; but millenarianism is a natural extension of the fundamentalist position, especially when applied to books like Ezekiel, Daniel and Revelation. It was historically important in the origins of modern fundamentalism, is enshrined in a standard text like the Scofield Bible, and is warmly espoused by many of the great evangelists who are idolised in fundamentalism. Fundamentalist millenarian schemes usually involve a periodisation of history, the idea that the true Church is a totally invisible entity, and the expectation that the age of the Church will be succeeded by another in which the Church will be replaced by a restored Jewish kingdom as the medium of God's government of the world. The reference of biblical texts is then distributed over the various ages or dispensations to which they are supposed to be relevant. One startling result of this is that central texts like the Sermon on the Mount are supposed not to be applicable to the age of the Church. Eschatological signs are discerned in events of history, especially in the Near East: these herald Armageddon and the end of the world. This eschatology is commonly supernaturalistic and deterministic, and totally disconnected from the life and the pressures of the visible Church in this world. Though many fundamentalists do not embrace millenarianism, they tolerate it as an accepted variation, and many of their leaders are strongly committed to it. It is in fact a good index of the ramifications of a fundamentalist understanding of Scripture.

SUMMARY

To sum up, Scripture is deeply loved in fundamentalism: the devotion to it is intense. Our criticism of it is not that it is too exclusively devoted to Scripture but that, out of understandable devotion to a traditional dogmatic position *about* the nature of Scripture in general, it has refused to be led by new understandings which have arisen from the evidence of Scripture itself and which require these older general understandings to be reassessed. Seeking above all things to be biblical, it has actually greatly straitened its own access to the actualities of Scripture. That is the tragedy of fundamentalism.

Alexandre Ganoczy

The Biblical Basis for the Dogmatic Way of Speaking

IT IS almost taken for granted by dogmatic theologians who are careful to take their scientific task seriously that they should keep pace with the discoveries made by exegetes. The relevant consensus of opinion about the interpretation of Scripture cuts through the different Christian confessions, in all of which there is also a strong resistance to a certain kind of 'scholastic' or 'manual' dogmatic theology, the exponents of which have used the Bible as a quarry for 'scriptural evidence'.[1] Dogmatic theologians who base their studies on biblical exegesis inevitably protest all the more strenuously against this method of *dicta probantia* if those who follow this method try to raise it to the level of the exclusive guardian of orthodoxy, 'pure doctrine' or 'the full truth of faith' and quote 'scriptural proofs' to this end.

1. THE PLACE OF 'SCRIPTURAL EVIDENCE'

What does 'scriptural evidence' mean in a traditional manual of dogmatic theology? It would seem to indicate a number of biblical texts quoted primarily with the aim of justifying in argument a thesis deduced from statements made for the most part by the Church's teaching office. The arguments used are mainly taken from the patristic 'tradition' and from rational, speculative philosophy. Apart from the method, something else is also expressed in this listing of biblical texts. It is the theological conviction, which has been regarded since time immemorial as valid, that first place should be given to Scripture as the form through which God's revelation has been mediated to man and the Christian identity of faith is expressed. Paul, who had received a rabbinical training, quoted the Pentateuch and the Old Testament prophets because of this conviction (see, for example, Gal. 3:6-18; 4:27-31; Rom. 4), with the aim of 'proving' the 'thesis' that Jesus Christ was the fulfilment of all God's promises. Every exegete, of course, knows that he imputed a deeper meaning to the words in the texts that he cited than they really contained (see, for example, Gal. 4:21-30; 1 Cor. 10:1-11) and that he even changed the wording quite considerably in certain cases (in 1 Cor. 15:55, for instance). If we were to judge Paul's use of 'scriptural evidence' by modern standards, we would without difficulty be able to accuse him in many cases of a 'Christological manipulation' of Old Testament statements.[2]

If, however, we were to apply this judgment, we would be guilty of committing a scientific and theoretical anachronism. We would also be failing to recognise an important aspect of Christian knowledge that is expressed in the procedure used by Paul. This is that, in his realisation of man's salvation, God has a historical plan,[3] the meaning of which was present 'in a hidden way' in the Old Testament and was first 'made manifest'[4] in the New Testament event of Christ. This knowledge of faith provides an objective justification for the superiority of the theologian in his association with Scripture as the 'letter'. The individual scriptural statement can and should be in accordance with this event of salvation in Jesus Christ and it should therefore also be placed at the disposal of the proclamation of that event.

This superiority of the believer to Scripture and the fact that he is also bound to Scripture are both subject now, in modern times, to very different conditions. Speaking about God is no longer exclusively regarded as confession, proclamation, doxology, wisdom and apologetics. It is also faced with a strictly scientific demand which includes a historical and critical understanding of history. This has resulted in the emergence of entirely new conditions governing theology and its expression of the mystery of Christ. The distinctively modern 'respect for history' (which was first stressed by Adolf von Harnack) and the ethos of the highest possible degree of accuracy and objectivity that accompanies that respect call for a radical reappraisal of the traditional use in dogmatic theology of 'scriptural evidence'. If this epoch-making change in the hermeneutical climate is not taken into account by dogmatic theologians, there is, as Karl Rahner has pointed out,[5] the possible danger of the use of a 'formal and logical extortion with regard to individual and isolated biblical statements', with which individual arguments, detached from their Christological centre, are shored up.

2. WHAT IS THE MEANING OF 'SCRIPTURAL EVIDENCE' TODAY?

In view of the present position in theological knowledge and understanding, especially in the West, the minimum scientific requirement is that a relative value should be given to the evidence as such provided by the so-called 'scriptural proofs'. In the form in which they are used in many manuals of theology, they either prove nothing at all to the reader today or else try to force an already open door in a way that is detrimental to faith. They also give rise to a lack of trust in a theology which at least has the apparent intention of binding the existential expression of man's faith in the Christian revelation to statements which are maintained in an interpretation which has already been proved wrong by modern biblical theology. The words 'scriptural evidence', then, may have erected a formal linguistic barrier and they have therefore to be withdrawn from circulation. This does not necessarily mean that we should dispense with the content expressed by a concrete 'scriptural proof'. To the extent that this content is in accordance with a lasting Christian conviction, attempts should be made to discover its fundamental intention and meaning and to represent it in a way that is intelligible to modern man.

Going beyond the terminological problem, however, the question arises as to what positive meaning the frequently misunderstood words 'scriptural evidence' may have today. We will consider this question in the following five sub-sections.

(a) The Whole of Scripture . . .

In the first place, the matter to which these words 'scriptural evidence' point is to be found in the assertion of the primacy of the whole of Scripture over all other ways of religious knowledge. The Fathers of the Second Vatican Council declared that the

Church 'has always regarded the Scriptures . . . as the supreme rule of faith', because 'they impart the word of God himself without change. . . . Therefore, like the Christian religion itself, all the preaching of the Church must be nourished and ruled by sacred Scripture'.[6]

(b) . . . in its Pluriformity

In the second place, it must be borne in mind that the Bible does not carry out its function of primacy nowadays without regard to the knowledge gained from the criticism of tradition and the text that it is above all a collection of testimonies of faith that have developed historically. It is this Bible that has become known to us through the achievements of modern exegesis which the Church claims to be 'the supreme rule of faith' imparting 'the word of God himself' in human words. Exegetes have provided indisputable evidence that the canonical books of the Bible[7] are very different from each other and are even in a dynamic relationship of polarity with each other, not only in their various literary genres, but also in their existential context within the history of traditions and in their intention and meaning. This fact therefore forms an essential part of the dynamism of Scripture with its power to prove, provide evidence or, even better, bear witness. It gives support to the dogmatically relevant idea that it was perfectly natural for the God of Jesus Christ to follow very pluriform ways in his revelation. This idea can be expressed even more clearly: the Bible, in the pluriformity of its traditions, shows itself to be normative. The Second Vatican Council did not declare this fact quite so explicitly, but it said clearly enough that 'truth is proposed and expressed in a variety of ways, depending on whether the text is history of one kind or another or whether its form is that of prophecy, poetry or some other type of speech'.[8] By the very fact of drawing attention to the special situation and intention of each author or editor of the Scripture in question, the Constitution on Revelation of Vatican II declared itself to be opposed to using Scripture in order to give support to later theses by drawing on isolated 'proofs' found in the texts of certain individual biblical authors.

(c) The 'Interactive' Function of Tradition

This does not mean that the individual biblical author is isolated from his ecclesial context and canonised. It is, on the contrary, assumed as a matter of course that he was borne up by a communal tradition to which he had given a literary expression. The history of traditions and the history of written Scripture came together interactively in this way. Scripture came about in this process in an extremely complex relationship. A highly pluriform communal and personal experience is at the basis of the texts which bear witness to Jesus Christ. This interweaving of different sources has made its own contribution to the interpretation of faith within the Bible itself.[9] In many cases, for example, biblical authors took the interpretation of Christ provided by other authors into account as well as his own situation with regard to the proclamation of the message.

This 'interaction' played a very important part in the formation of the canon of Scripture. This process took place in a very distinctive pattern of interactivity between *traditio* and *scriptura*, in other words, between the handing down of the faith that was alive in the Christian communities and centred on Jesus as crucified and raised from the dead on the one hand and the texts composed by certain witnesses to that faith on the other. Modern scriptural scholarship has shown that there was both an appropriation and an elimination of material in this entirely ecclesial process and that the Church was, in forming the canon, both 'self-regulating' and 'self-guiding'.

Our knowledge of the complex way in which the Bible evolved is of fundamental importance for hermeneutics in the Church today. Although the *traditio* of the present

Church community no longer has a function in forming a scriptural canon, it still has a function in handing on and interpreting Scripture (*traditio tradens et interpretans*). In this function that the Church exercises today, it is important that contact with the existing canonical scriptures should not be lost and that the task of interpretation should not go astray in the direction of many different *traditiones humanae*, as the Reformers called them. Surely the pronouncement made by the Second Vatican Council, that 'the Scriptures together with sacred tradition' are 'the supreme rule of faith' in the Church,[10] ought to be understood in this sense. It is obvious that what we have here is the Bible read in the light of scientific and exegetical knowledge. This is the Bible, hermeneutically 'together with' the tradition of the preaching, proclaiming and practising Church, which should appear today.

(d) *The Bible as a Foundation*

Present-day dogmatic theologians will also, of course, want to bear this situation in mind when they follow their customary scientific and ecclesial thought-processes in a consideration of faith in the light of the findings of biblical scholarship. If they do this consistently and honestly, they ought at the same time to be able to do justice to another aspect of what is meant by 'scriptural evidence' today. They will accept in their research a Bible that has been investigated in all its vital complexity as the foundation of their own work, which is co clearly directed towards life today. The Constitution on Revelation, *Dei Verbum*, expresses this important idea in the following way: 'Sacred theology rests on the written word of God . . . as its primary and perpetual foundation'.[11] Exegesis is the scientific study of this foundation and therefore can be accepted as what J. Blank called the 'basic science' of all the other theological disciplines.

(e) *No Absolute Value*

What we have just said can be misunderstood if it is seen as an attempt to give an absolute value to the (or to any) method of historical criticism or to the Jesus of the New Testament. Theology is, after all, not in the last resort based on exegesis and its frequently contradictory results or theories and opinions. This ultimate foundation is provided exclusively by the Word of God pronounced at the end of time and made tangible in Jesus Christ, that eschatological word to which the Bible, which is known to us in its original vitality through scientific study, bears witness. If we acknowledge the truth of this, we are bound to recognise that the scientific study of the Bible has an essential preparatory function. In the first place, by presenting the true face of the 'written Word of God' again and again to those working in other disciplines as an original model, it prepares the way for their work. In the second place, it also makes the task of the Church's teaching office fruitful. According to the Constitution on Revelation, 'It is the task of exegetes to work . . . towards a better understanding and explanation of the meaning of sacred Scripture, so that through preparatory study (*quasi praeparato studio*) the judgment of the Church may mature'.[12] It is also possible, then, to speak in this context of the 'primacy' of the Bible in the sense of 'scriptural evidence'.

3. EXEGESIS AND DOGMATIC THEOLOGY

If we consider the situation in which theology is placed today, we are at once confronted with the special problem of the relationship between exegesis and dogmatic theology. Many exegetes are still critical of dogmatic theologians for devoting more energy to their attempts to legitimise existing doctrines than to a patient consideration of the results of the scientific study of the Bible. On the other hand, exegetes are also criticised for losing themselves in details and apparently trivial controversy, for being reluctant to take biblical theology and hermeneutics sufficiently seriously and for failing to appreciate the ecclesial aspects and the pastoral use of the results of their work. In other words, the theory that we have outlined above does not seem to have become part of an interdisciplinary praxis.

The problem is extremely complex and all that I can do here is to touch on a few possible solutions. Exegetes and dogmatic theologians have been encouraged—notably in the Constitution on Revelation—to 'work diligently together'.[13] Their first task, then, is to become conscious of their own methods and themes. When they have reached this point, they will be better equipped to collaborate in the evolution of an ecclesial form of hermeneutics that will do justice to the historical nature of revelation. What is required, then, is a consciousness of the methods and themes of exegesis and dogmatic theology and the difference between them so that this can be placed at the service of the interpretation of the Word of God expressed in and through Christ, a task which has to be done, not separately, but together.

(a) Differences in Attitudes towards the History of the Church and its Dogmas

The first and most striking difference between the exegetical and the dogmatic interpretation of the Bible is that the first is only concerned with the phase in the history of salvation covered by the Bible, whereas the second deals with all the post-biblical phases. The dogmatic theologian cannot, for example, overlook the history of the Church and its dogmas that has taken place since the formation of the canon of Scripture, whereas the exegete not only can, but also must ignore this later history. He enjoys a considerable and legitimate freedom from dogma. In this fundamental freedom from dogmatic bonds, exegetes are able to make full use of the discoveries made and the means employed by the modern scientific study of history and language and in this way to do justice to the historical and literary aspects of the texts that they are studying. The dogmatic theologian, on the other hand, cannot let himself be completely bound by these aspects. He is committed to the task of finding a synthesis and of obtaining an overall view of the unity underlying the different individual theologies that are present in the Bible. He has therefore to conduct his hermeneutical investigations systematically and with particular concentration on themes. In this quest, he has, however, also to take care to bear in mind the distinctive character of the particular theology that is presented by each biblical author and to avoid any theological 'cocktail' of synoptic, Pauline and Johannine pronouncements. If he passes the test of this difficult ridge walk, the dogmatic theologian will satisfy the ideal of making the 'historical differentiation fruitful for a materially relevant view of the whole'.[14]

(b) Differences in the Point of Departure

For understandable reasons, the exegete begins at the bottom, by analysing the text in an attempt to gain an exact knowledge of the conditions governing its coming into being and what it aims to say. The dogmatic theologian, on the other hand, is less analytical and descriptive in his approach and more synthetic. He has to examine a biblical text or tradition for its ability to justify the truth of faith and to give permanent direction to the expression of faith in the individual and in the Church. In this context, the dogmatic theologian might be called the guardian of the 'canon in the canon', because he has again and again to call to mind the Christological 'centre of Scripture', by giving attention to its specifically Jesuanic elements.

(c) Different Responsibilities towards the Present

It is important to draw attention here to another division of labour between the dogmatic theologian and the exegete. Unlike the latter, the dogmatic theologian is directly responsible for the justification of faith here and now. It is essentially a part of his work to look for the signs of the times in which he is living, to question the conditions governing human life, thought, suffering and hope today and even to provide answers to these questions. His hermeneutics are directed not only towards a diachronic correlation (the biblical foundation and the history of dogma), but also towards a synchronic correlation. He has to listen to the times in which he is living in order to address them and to learn from the world in which he is living in order to teach it. The exegete, on the other hand, has first of all to do justice to his historical task by investigating and evaluating the normative period of the history of Christianity, including, for example, what Karlheinz Müller has called the 'orientation of Jesus of Nazareth's will', although this cannot, of course, take place completely independently of the great problems of the present time. He does not, however, have to attempt to find a solution to these problems in as direct a way as the dogmatic theologian has to.

(d) Different Attitudes towards the Church

There is finally a methodological difference in the attitude of exegetes towards the Church and that of dogmatic theologians. Whereas the exegete is able to ignore the post-biblical phase in the history of the Church and its dogmas and indeed has, in one respect, to do this, the dogmatic theologian has to bear in mind the doctrines that have developed in the course of the history of the Church as well as the need to consider and formulate doctrine here and now. In his examination of the Church's doctrines, however, he uses the same historical and critical method as that followed by the exegete in his investigation of the Bible. This method is completely indispensable to modern hermeneutics.

What emerges most clearly from the foregoing very fragmentary considerations of the specific tasks of both disciplines or, as F. Hahn has called exegesis and dogmatic theology, the two 'focal points of the science of theology', is their total dependence on each other. There can, in other words, be no 'basic science' or 'foundation science' without a 'constructive science' forming a superstructure and no 'preparation' without a continuation or continuation without a preparation. Finally, the one hermeneutical task of Christian faith has to be carried out, but the exegete and the dogmatic theologian each has his specific and specialised part to play in this task.

4. THE LIMITATIONS OF SCRIPTURE

In conclusion, I should like to say something about the inevitable limitations of this 'exposition of Scripture' of which the biblically based dogmatic theology outlined above consists. The Bible itself is limited, both in the light of the inexpressible mystery of God and in the light of its own centre, that of Jesus Christ himself. Revelation does not, after all, coincide with Scripture and the Word of God cannot be completely expressed in human words. God's revelation of himself is made known to man both in 'deeds and words'[15] and began with the active word of the creation of the world and continued with the 'non-verbal' testimonies of Jesus, with the result that even the most sacred written form of this revelation may have a relative character. All our exegetical and dogmatic pronouncements are therefore even more subject to the limitations of human and temporal relativity.

The dogmatic theologian who wishes to proceed scientifically in this way is therefore committed to a very modest task. Like the biblical exegete, he cannot rest content with the 'written Word of God'. Even from the human vantage-point of man's experience of reality in the world, however, the dynamic power of the unwritten, ever new mystery of God forces itself again and again on the theologian who works 'in accordance with Scripture'—one has only to think, in this connection, of the anthropological mysteries of love and hate, that can never be completely grasped in symbolic terms. In this secular and pastoral respect, however, certain open questions have also to be taken into consideration, vital questions which cannot be ignored by theologians and which dogmatic theologians in particular are not necessarily able to refer to biblical scholars and the Bible itself.[16]

Translated by David Smith

Notes

1. See the positions taken by the dogmatic theologians Hans Küng and Walter Kasper in *Theologische Quartalschrift* 159 (1979, 1) 24-36, 36-40 in respect of J. Blank's thesis on 'Exegese als theologische Basiswissenschaft', *ibid*. 2-23.

2 See P. Blaser 'Schriftbeweis. I: In der Schrift selbst' *Lexikon für Theologie und Kirche* 9 p. 484ff.

3. See the Dogmatic Constitution on Divine Revelation, *Dei Verbum*, 15.

4. *Ibid*. 16.

5. In his article on 'Schriftbeweis. II: In der systematischen Theologie' *Lexikon für Theologie und Kirche* 9 p. 487.

6. *Dei Verbum*, 21.

7. For the contemporary debate on the canon of Scripture, see *Theologische Quartalschrift* 159, cited in note 1, especially J. Blank, 7-13, 69f; W. Kasper, 38f and H. J. Vogt, 53f. See also the helpful observations of G. Ebeling *Studium der Theologie. Eine enzyklopädische Orientierung* (Tübingen 1975) p. 13-20.

8. *Dei Verbum*, 12, 1-4; see also 19.

9. Ebeling, in the work cited in note 7, p. 15.

10. *Dei Verbum*, 21.

11. *Dei Verbum*, 24.

12. *Dei Verbum*, 12, 5.

13. *Dei Verbum*, 23.

14. Ebeling, in the work cited in note 7, p. 22.

15. *Dei Verbum*, 2, 17, 19, which provide evidence of the conviction of the Fathers of the Second Vatican Council that revelation took place not only in words, but also and especially in Jesus' actions or in acts of divine love.

16. Karl Rahner says, in his article on 'Biblische Theologie und Dogmatik' *Lexikon für Theologie und Kirche* 2 p. 440, that dogmatic theologians have 'to ask Scripture questions' which are not necessarily questions concerning biblical theology.

DOCUMENTATION

Hans Küng

A Letter on
Christology and Infallibility

Foreword

While this issue of *Concilium* was being prepared, Hans Küng was deprived of the *missio canonica* by order of the Roman Congregation for the Doctrine of Faith. The debate prompted by this decision is not least a 'dispute about the interpretation of the Bible', and it is on account of the theological issues inherent in, and the world-wide repercussions stemming from, this case that we venture to print the letter of 12 February 1980 to Dr George Moser, Bishop of Rottenburg-Stuttgart, in which Hans Küng commented on the main issues of the controversy. This topical example makes it plain just how little the historical-critical interpretation of Scripture and the relationship between Bible and Church, exegesis and dogmatics, theology and magisterium are purely academic questions. We have omitted the third part of the letter, which deals with legal questions pertaining to the resolution of the conflict. Since the letter was written a solution has been found within the University of Tübingen itself which leaves Hans Küng in possession of the chair of ecumenical theology and of the directorship of the Institute of Ecumenical Research, even though no longer under the aegis of the Faculty of Catholic Theology but under the direct charge of the President and Senate of the University (on the general context, see *Der Fall Küng. Eine Dokumentation* ed. N. Greinacher and H. Haag (Munich 1980).

My Lord Bishop,

Since your return from Rome on 29 December 1979 a menacing situation has developed on account of your decision to deprive me of the *missio canonica* and to seek 'redress' from the State. Believers, pastors and theologians, along with entire congregations, Catholic groupings, associations and faculties have been seized by a deep disquiet about the development of our Catholic Church, latent polarisations have openly erupted and there is talk on all sides of an impending crisis. I take this whole grave development with the utmost seriousness and for this reason I now address you.

For I am convinced that an unprejudiced and above all a competent theological dialogue can at least serve to shed light on what is alleged to make my Catholicity appear doubtful in the eyes of certain ecclesiastical authorities. With reference to such a clarification I wish to begin here by setting the record straight on both Christology and infallibility, then to speak of my actual theological intentions and finally to say something about the appropriate formulae.

1. CHRISTOLOGY

Corrections

The assertion that I have not clearly affirmed Jesus' *divine Sonship* as understood in Scripture and tradition, that I have misrepresented this doctrine, or that I have expounded it in a sense foreign to the Church is incorrect and cannot be proved from my writings.

The assertion that I have disputed the permanent *binding force* of the Christological statements of the Councils of Nicaea and Chalcedon for the Catholic Church is incorrect and can be positively refuted from my writings.

Therefore the assertion that it is impossible for me in terms of my theology to say an unmistakeable Yes to the Church's *confession of faith* is also incorrect and—in view of my various writings on Christology—incomprehensible. As everyone who either knows me, has carefully read my books or has heard my lectures is aware, I say a resolute Yes to the Church's confession of faith and shall continue to do so, above all in the liturgy as the proper setting of the Credo. Nor do I have anything against the interpretation of Jesus' divine Sonship achieved by the fourth and fifth centuries as such, an attitude which is entirely consonant with my writings and with the detailed analyses of my book *Menschwerdung Gottes*.

Therefore the *connection* established by the Roman document, in company with the pulpit message and statement issued by the German bishops, between my inquiry into the problem of *infallibility* and my statements on *Christology* also strikes me as incorrect and—in the light of my theological work as a whole—as meaningless. According to the episcopal statement of 7 January 1980 the 'defects' in my understanding of infallibility are disclosed in my 'utterances on the person of Jesus Christ'. This assertion is entirely unwarranted and wakens the suspicion that I practise Christology by dealing recklessly with the binding statements of Scripture and tradition and even that I work out my Christology at their expense.

The impression created by the German bishops that according to my theology it is '*not God himself* who has turned to man in Jesus Christ' is therefore misleading and in violation of my decisive intentions. On the contrary, one of the fundamental Christological propositions of my book *Existiert Gott?* runs as follows: 'We meet with God himself in a unique and definitive way in the person and work of Jesus' (p. 749). Hence it would be entirely possible for this sentence from the pulpit message jointly issued by the German bishops to have come from my pen: 'If God himself did not turn to man in Jesus Christ, then Jesus is not able to redeem us from sin and death'.

In this connection I must vigorously call attention to the fact that—as I am bound to infer from its chairman's letter—the German Bishops' Conference has not even taken note of my detailed testimony to Christ in *Existiert Gott?*, a section of this work which contains the clarifications promised during my Stuttgart conversation with yourself and Cardinals Höffner and Volk. Any proper investigation would have found it absolutely mandatory to take cognisance of this book along with the others. For the rest, my Lord Bishop, I am sure you share my conviction that the various bodies and authorities in the Church leadership who have given rise to these mistaken interpretations of my theology also stand under the moral obligation of remedying these misrepresentations.

My basic concerns

As you, my Lord Bishop, are aware, the fact that a legitimate plurality exists within

Catholic Christology has been demonstrated by all the discussions of the past years. You are moreover aware that the *theological difficulties* do not end but only begin with the profession of the fundamental and universally binding credal statements of the Church. And you surely also share my opinion that the task of theologians in the face of these difficulties—with which theological literature everywhere is replete—is to grapple with them in such a way that, on the one hand, the meaning of these credal statements is preserved while, on the other, the man of today is enabled to appreciate them afresh.

It is undisputed among Catholic theologians that theology has the right and the duty to take into its service all *methods* which are suitable for research into and exposition of the faith. And it is likewise undisputed that this practice will necessarily result in theology's constantly discovering new ways of putting things. The ecclesiastical censures suffered by Thomas Aquinas and, in our century, the Papal Biblical Commission's condemnations of the historical-critical method are simply outstandingly blatant examples of the tendency of novel formulations to start their course as objects of controversy. Many novel formulations have nevertheless prevailed because their truth content has contained the seed of future victory. Conversely, many old formulations have not held their ground, despite official sanction, if they have proved scientifically and pastorally unsuitable.

It is therefore my conviction that what is at stake in the present conflict is not the Christian *substance*, which is common property, but the *manner* in which we can express it today. My starting-point remains that our common faith in Jesus Christ must be expressed in such a way as to be understandable not only to practising Catholic or Protestant Christians, but also to the countless inquirers outside the Church. In order to avoid unnecessary polarisations and conflicts within the Church it is fitting that both bishops and theologians should be seen to engage in this enterprise, which may not be pursued at the expense of Christian truth.

Hence it is also clear that the present debate cannot begin by considering specific statements, but should start with the overall context of a theological programme, with its methodological premises and its actual goals. Only against such a background will it be possible to form a well-founded judgment about specific statements. It is for this reason that I wish to set before you some fundamental indications of the methodological and hermeneutical premises of my statements on Christology.

(*a*) *My first concern is a consistent, scripturally oriented theology.* According to the Second Vatican Council Scripture ought once more to become the '*soul of theology*'. It is therefore right to take Scripture seriously as the decisive and ever present source of Church tradition and to have it bear fruit for contemporary proclamation and theology through a 'mediated immediacy', an entirely legitimate technique which has been practised continually in Church history. In this enterprise I place myself in the tradition of those great Catholic theologians who have understood theology as '*scientia de dinina pagina*' (Thomas Aquinas). Such fresh listening to Scripture permits us continually to experience the astonishing inspirational and disquieting power of this fundamental witness to our faith which always resists being completely packaged and pigeon-holed in our systematic categories. Scripture has continually exercised such a critical-productive function *vis-à-vis* the faith of the Church and will continue to do so.

Presupposing such a use of the Bible, I wish to defend myself against the allegation that a scripturally oriented theology of this kind confronts the 'Church's interpretation of the faith' with a 'historical-critical understanding of the Bible'. What is at stake here is nothing other than the interpretation of Scripture with the best possible methods available to us at the present day. The Encyclical *Divino Afflante Spiritu* of 1943 and the Second Vatican Council frankly commit the Catholic exegete to the historical-critical method. I have taken this method seriously in the field of dogmatics and in the discussion about my Christology no exegete of note has maintained that I do not have a broad exegetical consensus behind me on the central issues. This fact encourages me to take the path I do, yet it has hardly been sufficiently pondered in the discussion, which has been directed chiefly by dogmaticians. I wish expressly to implore you too, my Lord Bishop, to reflect on this fact yet again. While many people are inclined to reproach me with playing off Scripture against tradition, my concern has only been to ward off the much greater danger of tradition being played off against Scripture or of the power of the scriptural witness over against tradition only being felt to a limited extent. A tradition which is not in keeping with Scripture is not Catholic.

(b) *My second concern is a consistent, historically warranted theology*. That I do not stand alone in my advocacy of this programme is demonstrated by the fact that the historical relativity of credal statements and even of the earliest witnesses of the faith preserved in Scripture is no longer denied by anyone. Even the Roman statement *Mysterium Ecclesiae* of 1973 paid due attention to this factor. Anyone who thinks historically immediately discovers that such things as 'Church', 'tradition', 'unfolding of faith', 'development of dogma' and the general necessity of continually ensuring one's Christian identity afresh through binding credal statements are deeply human phenomena and entirely in keeping with the nature of man.

Credal statements therefore cannot simply be repeated, least of all by theologians. In this context we are right to put our trust in the Spirit who continually leads us anew into the truth, which is nothing but the 'old' truth of Jesus Christ himself. Anyone who thinks historically must therefore expose himself to precisely those questions which are posed to him from the perspective of the origins of Christian history and of the Christian Church. Each confession of faith, along with each Council and each statement later made by either the teaching office or a qualified theologian, must be legitimised in terms of the original message. This is particularly clear in the case of the first ecumenical Council of Nicaea which, in the absence of any 'intermediate authorities' in the shape of other Councils, made a decisive appeal to Scripture, whence it established its own authority. The tension between origin (viz., the original biblical tradition, *'norma normans'*) and 'tradition' (viz., derived, post-biblical tradition, *'norma normata'*) must remain. It may not be defused by any static model of explanation, organic model of development or dialectical model of speculation. The original Christian message remains outside our control, nor can we ever neatly package and pigeon-hole it or reduce it to a trite formula, for it continually is and remains a future reality, in which respect it is closely bound up with the new forms of Christian lifestyle which are in vogue at any given time.

Anyone who thinks historically will therefore be aware that, despite the existence of a binding Canon and of binding doctrinal pronouncements and without denying the binding force of earlier statements of the faith, we can neither predict nor stipulate in advance either the path which further reflection on the faith will take or the linguistic form in which it will be expressed. The historical dialectic of continuity and discontinuity frankly forbids any *a priori* separation of abiding from transitory, essential from inessential, or kernel from husk. As in the past, the faith will continue to be couched in fresh terms and new overall theological blueprints will continue to be developed. And we shall continue to stand anew before the problem of the emergence of new 'paradigms' and 'models of understanding' of the faith which begin life as objects of controversy.

Anyone who thinks historically therefore has some understanding for the awkward situation in which disputes about orthodoxy can get enmeshed. People can easily talk 'past one another' and yet be unable to prevent many committed Christians from taking up the position in question, accepting it as an entirely new opportunity and sensing in it an agent of liberation which makes possible a new Christian faith.

I am convinced that we stand in just such a period of transition, and I am disposed to see such books of mine as *The Church* and—*par excellence*—*On Being a Christian* and *Existiert Gott?* in the context of a new Christian experience of reality, evidence of which can be seen in the deep unrest displayed by many clergymen and R.E. teachers in the past few weeks. Having long been in preparation, this new experience of reality is now slowly making headway even though as yet unable to establish its complete legitimacy—unless such validity is in fact conferred by its propinquity to the original Christian message, to Jesus' proclamation, activity, destiny and person. The needs of a theology involved in such a transition, my Lord Bishop, are not restricted to a continuous scrutiny of its orthodoxy. It has a much greater need of trust, encouragement and brotherly goodwill. For this reason it also requires the recognition of its own self-understanding. That is to say, if a theologian understands himself to be a Catholic, then the proper initial reaction is to take him seriously precisely as a Catholic theologian, even in the event of his arriving at unusual, albeit well reasoned, conclusions. *In that case he also enjoys the right of abode in this Church until his non-Catholicity is proved by argument.* Hence he enjoys the right of abode in this Church until his own, hitherto unusual, arguments are refuted in terms of the original Christian message. Since our Church has so often begun by condemning things which later acquired the right of abode, we ought today to exercise a double measure of caution.

(c) *My third concern is a theology which unreservedly welcomes the questions of the present day.* That is to say, every theologian should live in brotherly solidarity with the men of his age. I am convinced that, just as he is obliged before God to become a Jew to the Jews and a Greek to the Greeks, so by the same token he has a duty towards *the men of the present day*—including the inquiring, the sceptical, the despairing and those who are disappointed with the Church—to become a man with the questions, hopes and fears of the present day.

All these things are especially true with reference to questions of Christology, where the Christian faith is still largely dominated by a world picture which has lost its relevance. B. Welte is one of the few Catholic theologians who demands at the present time that the appropriate conclusions be drawn with respect to a future Christology: 'Does this mean that there is a complete rupture in the continuity of the Christian self-understanding and, accordingly, in the continuity of our understanding of Jesus, of Christology? We shall be obliged to say that there is indeed a rupture in continuity with respect to the *form* of our speaking, questioning and thinking. But there is not necessarily any rupture in continuity with respect to the *thing* at stake, hence in our case to Jesus and his gospel, that is, to the words which proclaim him. Thus the witness to Jesus will continue to be conveyed to us through the old words, for example the words of Holy Scripture and also the words of the Church and its confessional formulae. These words continually declare afresh the Jesus thing, which is itself old and yet ever new. But the old words and hence the old cause will now be questioned and understood from the perspective of a new world and hence of a new language and of new horizons of inquiry, in which they will take on a new form for a new epoch.'

Welte therefore proposes that theological thought about Jesus should let '*event* replace *ousia/substantia* as its leading category'. I have endeavoured to think along these lines myself in the company of many exegetes. Welte continues: 'Therefore we still share the Councils' basic intention, namely to expound Scripture, even when our thinking carries us beyond their form. The man Jesus *occurred*, he expressed the incomparable reality of his self and his spirit in word, deed and destiny, thereby having a multiple effect on those who heeded him and producing an echo in those thus affected. We can label all this the *event* of Jesus or the occurrence of the history of Jesus. A unique and entire man occurred in this event or history, and in one and the same event there occurred the entire and unique God. That is, he announced himself to man in a new way, in judgment and redemption, in this event or history of Jesus. Should we attempt to think in terms of this conceptual blueprint, then we shall once again be faced with the unity of the divine and the human, yet this will no longer be thought of as a static essence but rather as an event in motion. In this way the basic biblical intention of the ancient confessional formulae has been safeguarded, but the manner and form of their thinking has been changed.'

If a theologian attempts in this way to speak in categories of event, occurrence and revelation, then it is inappropriate to wish to measure him by or even to condemn him with categories of essence. The proposition that God himself is definitively and unsurpassably revealed in Jesus' person is accordingly no less full-blooded than the earlier proposition that Jesus 'is' God. Karl Rahner has just recently reminded us of the great ambiguity of the little word 'is' in this context. At the Würzburg Synod he 'publicly registered a certain protest' against some remarks of Cardinal Höffner: 'Cardinal Höffner said that Jesus of Nazareth *is* God. I rejoined that this is self-evidently a Christian, irreversible and finally binding truth. Yet this thesis can also be misunderstood. While other "is-statements" express a simple identity of subject and predicate, such an identity is emphatically *not* given between the humanity of Jesus and God's eternal Logos. There is *unity* here, but not *identity*. I only say this to make it clear that there are abiding questions and even differences of opinion within the Church and its orthodoxy on the subject of the Christological dogma. What I wish to make clear is this: I do not think that the question of the possible that Küng has raised in relation to Christology can be given quite so simple an answer as was perhaps offered in the Church's Cologne statement.' Though he is well known to be in disagreement with me on the question of infallibility, Rahner has, after minutely reading my book *On Being a Christian*, expressly confirmed that he 'could discover no absolute affront against a defined dogma in Christology'.

At this point there appears an unexpected and astonishing convergence between a modern personal-historical starting-point and the starting-point of the New Testament Christologies. It is precisely the New Testament that encourages us to work out a new statement of what the person and cause of Jesus mean to faith by using figures, symbols, metaphors, names and concepts which are understood today and are therefore in a position to act as a clarifying force. Precisely in this way the proclamation of faith in Jesus Christ remains creative and avoids the danger of becoming fossilised due to fear of surrendering some aspect of the true faith simply by couching it in different terms.

You will perhaps reply, my Lord Bishop, that such a theological programme opens the floodgates to arbitrary speculations. Since I am very well aware of this danger in a time of upheaval, I have devoted especial attention to this very question. This leads me to a last point.

(*d*) *My fourth concern is a theology which consistently sets forth the Christian faith in terms of Jesus Christ.* Hence my central and assuredly legitimate reply is that Jesus Christ himself constitutes what is unique in the Christian faith. The perpetual task of the Christian theologian is therefore to return an answer to the question, Who is this Jesus Christ? To put it more correctly, *Who is this Jesus of Nazareth* who for us believers is the Christ and the Son of God? Bearing in mind the difficulties which many people have with the traditional Christological statements, I have taken the path suggested by exegesis. That is to say, I have chosen the method of giving a scholarly account of the proclamation and lifestyle of Jesus of Nazareth, of the history of the influence which he exercised both before and after his death.

The systematic development of this methodological starting-point, of which I am not the sole advocate, has led to wide-ranging discussions. My critics, however, have tended to proceed from presuppositions which are not applicable to my methodological self-understanding. The outstanding example of this has been the officially enunciated insinuation that I consider a 'hypothetical historical reconstruction, on its own and independently of other factors, competent to offer adequate access to the theological understanding of Jesus Christ'. I have two points to make about this allegation.

First, this clouding of the basic issue by an imprecise use of theoretical scholarly terminology conceals the true question. The latter can be put as follows: Can we still know something about Jesus of Nazareth, who is certainly no myth? For our primary concern, irrespective of the plethora of problems to do with historical hermeneutics which arise in this context, is quite simply with the *report* about Jesus' person and cause, with the report of the experiences of this Jesus which the first believers had. This report has had an inalienable right of abode in the Catholic Church since time immemorial. And theologians have been able since time immemorial to proceed from the possibility and necessity for faith of a historical visualisation of this person Jesus. The fact that this historical question has, under the influence of a growing historical-critical consciousness, led to increasingly refined statements of the problem and interpretative possibilities speaks for rather than against this *report*.

Second, it is clear to every historian today that he cannot restrict his role to the reproduction of positive facts. For every text is couched and understood in terms of a *pre-understanding*. And every comprehensive interpretation of historical dates, persons or events invariably presupposes the interpreter's own point of view. It is accordingly irrelevant to confront him with the alternative *either* the historical Jesus *or* the faith of the Church. Why is this so?

The method of interpreting Jesus' person and cause certainly begins with the historically important sources and with the historically elucidated history of Jesus, a history which did not come to an end with his death but acquired a new quality through the Easter experiences. Yet this history was written by a believing theologian who stood before the questions: How and why can we rely at all on this Jesus of Nazareth? How and why is he able to stand before us and on our behalf in God's name? Is this in methodological terms a Christology 'from below'? Yes, but it is practised from the standpoint of one who believes in Jesus Christ. This Christology 'from below' could only be pursued so consistently and—for many—so convincingly because it was written by a believer. Hence historical reason does not block our access to God's revelation, but facilitates it.

I cannot deal here with the many specific questions which arise in connection with this attempt to rethink Christology. For example, does the historical approach tend to conceal and cloud over the proper challenge of Christianity? I believe that this is not the case and am convinced that it is only through a combination of historical distance and topical relevance that both the challenge and the non-simultaneity of the Christian message can once again be reconciled. Does the method of historical report and analysis render a believing, confessing Yes or No superfluous? I believe that this is not the case, for it is only through a historical presentation of the material that the alternative views and the central issues facing Christian belief once again become so specific as to issue a fresh challenge to decide. Does this method tend to produce doubt and unease? I believe that this is not the case and am convinced that it is only through this method that many people once again become clear about just what they can rely on in faith. Since it is the Jesus whom we confess as the Christ who gives our faith its proper identity, a Catholic theologian must be permitted to present him afresh as the great challenge issued to the men of today in church and society.

Credal formulae or credal structure?

On the basis of all that I have said above, my Lord Bishop, I wish to come back to the Christological questions which Cardinal Höffner put to me on 22 April 1977. In terms of the hermeneutical principles specified above, *I profess*—as I stated at the beginning of this letter—*the central Christological formulae of our confession of faith*.

If you bear this whole exceedingly complex range of problems in mind, my Lord Bishop, then perhaps you will have a better understanding of my reasons—quite apart from the issue of the *right* to ask such questions—for not wishing on that occasion to give pre-packaged replies to abbreviated, Catechism-like questions which merely suppress the actual theological-hermeneutical problem yet again. The epochal upheaval which has shaken the foundations of a whole category system, the extremely difficult task of interpreting the traditional Christological statements of the Creeds, and the increasing distress which many of those confronted with traditional Christology are facing in their personal faith form three reasons which lead me expressly to implore you and your brother bishops to take seriously my conviction—shared by many—that faith in Jesus Christ is neither weakened nor reduced to the level of provisional discourse about him in those statements of mine which have been the butt of episcopal censure. We share the same intentions and the same subject-matter, but we frame and formulate our belief differently. Everything hinges on these differing structures!

My insistence on this point is not motivated by any opinionatedness on my part but by fear lest all those who have learned to believe in Jesus Christ anew in the framework of a historical Christology be left to their own devices and relapse sooner or later into sceptical reservations. In that case the R.E. teachers and the pastors would be the ones left to bear the painful consequences. What is at stake here, even for me, is the link between theology and the Church. But an even greater reality is at stake, and that is the continuity of the substance captured in those binding statements. Credal formulae are also at stake, certainly, but only in the context of a particular structure of belief. These two factors must be considered together. Anyone who has understood this has, in my opinion, understood the conflict which the Catholic Church is going through at the present time (and not solely on my account!).

2. INFALLIBILITY

It is not necessary to go into such great detail on the problem of infallibility as was required by the Christological issues, although it too can only be solved in the framework of a broad theological programme. As you are aware, my Lord Bishop, this question has attracted relatively little attention in German-speaking countries, while as far as the Roman Congregation for the Doctrine of Faith is concerned it forms the crucial issue of the whole debate. It has here, after all, been called on to sit in judgment of its own case! It would thus be profitable if by mutual effort we could succeed in taking the heat out of this discussion and putting this problem into perspective. Let me then begin by setting the record straight.

Corrections

It has surely not remained hidden from you that the scope of my inquiry into the definition of infallibility has been *constantly widened* in the last few weeks and turned into a basic question about my relationship to Christian truth in general. Here too, in my opinion, I possess the right of protection by the ecclesiastical authorities against unjustified overinterpretations. For this reason I make the following points.

The assertion that I deny the *permanent binding force* of credal statements which demand an unmistakable Yes or No is incorrect and can be positively refuted from my writings. The assertion of certain interpreters that by affirming binding statements I reject 'ultimately binding' statements is incomprehensible and devoid of material foundation. There can surely be no upgrading of 'binding', properly understood!

Furthermore, the assertion that I brush aside Vatican I's definition of infallibility is incorrect and cannot be proved from my writings. For the fact of the matter is that the talk of *'revising'* Vatican I in my two latest publications occurred in highly distinctive circumstances. It took note, on the one hand, of the problem—raised by Yves Congar yet hardly discussed thus far—of the reception and 're-reception' of conciliar decisions and, on the other, of the results of recent historical scholarship. I shall comment further below on the meaning and significance of my 'inquiry'.

The sweeping assertion that the *'truth of Scripture'* is the real issue in the discussion with my 'inquiry' (so the German bishops' statement of 7 January 1980) is incorrect and runs completely counter to the fundamental intention of my theological work. Even so, I am willing to leave the judgment on this assertion to professional exegetes.

I find the assertion that I 'pre-eminently and much more fundamentally (cast doubt) on the Spirit-wrought gift of the Church's preservation in the truth of God' (*ibid.*) incomprehensible and diametrically at odds with my actual statements. For I have attached added weight to this very factor in connection with my 'inquiry'. I feel that the bishops are guilty of gravely misleading the public by printing only one of the writings impugned by Rome—viz., the *Foreword* to Hasler's book—in their documentation of my case, neglecting to include the *Theological Meditation* which I purposely published at the same time and expressly designated as a positive supplement to the *Foreword*. I completely and entirely affirm the idea outlined in the title *Church—preserved in the Truth*, and since the book aims to put flesh and bones on this concept it by no means comes to a halt with a 'sweeping' affirmation.

Finally, the assertion of the Roman statement of 15 January 1979 that I hold the teaching office in contempt and pit my own opinions against the Church's interpretation of the faith is wrong and has a disparaging ring. I have always presented my inquiries with supporting arguments, I have accepted the relevant constraints inherent in the theological search for truth and I have gone out of my way to provoke theological argument. Even my critics have conceded that difficult problems exist here which are not of my invention and which vitally affect the whole of Catholic theology.

You surely share my opinion, my Lord Bishop, that an objective dialogue is only possible if these corrections are respected by all sides and, if at all possible, brought to the notice of unsettled believers by the Church authorities. For in the case of infallibility too highly fundamental issues are at stake which can only be fruitfully discussed in a *wider overall context*. I therefore wish to refer once more to the underlying factors in terms of which I am convinced that the present dispute ought to be appraised.

My basic concerns

Let me simply once again recall the *four dimensions* in which my theological thought moves. The sequence in which I present them, by the way, is indicative of the method and content of my thought. It is also in the question of ecclesiastical infallibility that my theological thought intends:

  (i) to be consistently related to Scripture;
 (ii) to give a historical justification of its tenets in terms of Christian origins;
(iii) to accept the questions of the present day without reservation; and
(iv) to bring Jesus, whom we confess as the Christ, to bear as the decisive criterion of our faith in word and deed.

My inquiry moves within the framework supplied by these dimensions, as do the hypotheses which I myself have proposed as solutions of the problem. I do not wish to deal with them here since the arguments have been public knowledge for a long time.

You will retort that I have thus far paid no heed to the decisive dimension which contemporary Catholic theology deems so essential: *ecclesiality*. I wish to reply that ecclesiality is consummated in all the dimensions enumerated above. For I am concerned with the Apostolic Church (relationships to Scripture), with the temporal Catholicity of this Church (historical justification), with its spatial Catholicity (demands of the present day) and, finally, with the conviction that we are the Church of Jesus Christ (Jesus Christ as decisive criterion). Now the principal issues around which the infallibility debate has tended to resolve have had to do with the concept of a visible Church which can be identified through *particular offices and credal propositions*. Let me give some indication of what I mean.

(a) *I am concerned to serve the cause of uniting the separated Churches*. This aspect has been conspicuous by its *almost complete absence* from the discussions with the Roman authorities and from the various statements issued in Germany over the last few weeks. The suspicion has simply been expressed that I am pursuing an ecumenism which neglects the question of truth.

But this judgment fails to come to grips with the true *importance* of the ecumenical problem. All the non-Catholic churches regard the dogma of infallibility as a doctrine of recent origin peculiar to Roman Catholicism. And it is precisely when they are in principle prepared to acknowledge the Petrine ministry of the Bishop of Rome that all the non-Catholic churches are disposed to see in this dogma one of the chief obstacles in the path of a possible reunion.

It is therefore the *duty* of a theologian committed to ecumenical theology, who is moreover the Director of an Institute for Ecumenical Research, to take up this difficult problem and think it through in a self-critical manner in the light of the inquiries addressed to us from outside the Catholic Church. This is the only effective way of furthering the ecumenical cause in this crucial area.

The widely documented *dismay* presently felt by numerous non-Catholic colleagues all over the world shows just how much the credibility of our Church depends on the resolute reappraisal of this problem. Even in the statement signed by numerous professors from Catholic Theological Faculties in Germany we read as follows: 'If Catholic theology no longer possesses the freedom to pose questions from the developed present to the originating past, in order to reopen lost opportunities for unity and union, then it will be responsible for pulling the rug from under the feet of the ecumenical theological dialogue. In this case, however, the Church's ecumenical endeavour would lose its whole credibility and the previous development would be bound to grind to a halt.' No one in our Church can have any interest in such a state of affairs.

(b) *I am concerned to contribute to the clarification of the relationship between theology and the teaching office*. As you are aware, measured against the history of the Church and the faith, the dogma of infallibility was defined very late in the day. For many centuries there was no mention of the infallibility of the pope, and for several further centuries it made no appearance as a formal item of the criteriology of Catholic theology. From the middle ages onwards the self-understanding and function of a 'teaching office' was subjected to a *pronounced change*. Hence there is no reason to fear that a discussion of the infallibility issue will shake the foundations of the whole Catholic understanding of truth. A glance at Church history and at the other churches proves from the very outset that Christian truth already transmits a high degree of meaning, certainty and redemptive power through such channels as the witness of Scripture, the confession of faith, the tradition which is common to all churches and the faith which is lived out by Christian people.

My intention in pointing out this home truth is certainly not to pronounce the Petrine ministry superfluous! After all, I have continually striven to explain to non-Catholic

Christians the significance of this ministry for the Catholic Church and for ecumenical Christendom. Nor does the Petrine ministry advance a superfluous claim when it alleges that its service of preserving unity for the Catholic Church is realised, when necessary, by means of a binding language and of warding off errors. But this claim is only meaningful when it understands itself as serving the witness to the faith given by the Church as a whole. A dialectic must be upheld here which can free us from a great deal of anxiety. For while we all share the conviction that the Church stands in need of a unifying ministry of witness, we are at the same time obliged to remain in serious discussion concerning the degree of autonomy which ought to be conceded to theology within the Church.

The experience of our century has proved that a free theology committed to truth alone can render great service to *the Church's credibility*. But in view of the fact that many great theologians were originally either reprimanded or called to account, it is imperative for us today to succeed in breaking through the atmosphere of latent mistrust and in stating with increasing clarity the independent tasks which are proper to teaching office and theology respectively.

You are aware, my Lord Bishop, that in my inquiry into infallibility I proposed certain *hypotheses* and that I was in truth obliged to do so. Now these hypotheses were designed to loosen the problem and to explain to wider circles the legitimate concerns contained in this dogma. I do not maintain that I have succeeded in clarifying the relationship between teaching office and theology, and for this very reason I implore you to do all you can to enable this comprehensive issue to be comprehensively discussed without recourse to emotion or menacing sanctions. I consider that the above mentioned statement by German theologians backs me up in making this request: 'Theology must stake an unqualified claim to the opportunity, which pertains to its *inalienable freedom*, of proposing and testing hypotheses, settling controversies by way of reason and argument and correcting and surmounting errors through scholarly disputations. The more scholarly disputation can take place without let or hindrance, the more it will resist arbitrariness and serve the truth in virtue of the argumentative rigour which it will compel.'

The aim of the two foregoing sections was to describe the *background* which confers on the infallibility debate its inescapable urgency. It may be said that they are couched in very general terms and that they leave my own attitude towards the infallibility definition still undecided. For this reason I now add a third point:

(c) *I am concerned to clarify the meaning of and the reasons underlying the infallibility definition.* Now anyone who does not take the definition of papal infallibility seriously will not speak about it and yet still manage to practise theology. I myself take it with the *utmost seriousness* and since the early sixties I have endeavoured in all due respect to subject it to precise analysis and to expose its intention to the man of today in an intelligible fashion. The intensive discussion of the last decade has shown me, along with other Catholic theologians, a twofold problem:

(i) The data presented by *both exegesis and the history of doctrine* put serious difficulties in the way of any well-founded arguments in favour of the definition. Much has been written about these difficulties and they have been exhaustively discussed at several study conferences where I have volunteered to engage in debate. Reasons of space forbid me to devote closer attention to them in this letter.

(ii) Progress in our understanding of hermeneutics and the philosophy of language has rendered the *meaning of the infallibility definition* unclear. The fact of the matter is that definitions of material beliefs can constantly be translated and clarified afresh, that they can be expounded in the light of new questions and rethought in accordance with the most recent hermeneutical reflection. By way of contrast, the infallibility definition—hence a definition of the formal binding character of certain beliefs—itself posits a binding hermeneutic. The upshot of a changed hermeneutical awareness is to plunge the infallibility definition into a conflict of interpretation to which only brief allusion can be made here. For example, the infallibility definition is based on a legal hermeneutic. How then are new exegetical results to be brought to bear? And it exacerbates the issue of specific credal propositions ('propositions', 'judgments', 'definitions', 'sentences'). For how does it cope with the problem of comprehensive propositional units? Since it proceeds from the model of propositions which are infallibly true from the very outset, how is this to be squared with the genuine concern of theological scholarship to furnish good reasons for credal propositions, especially when we consider that the teaching office claims to be competent to pass judgment on interpretations independently of fresh arguments and that in such cases it constitutes the final court of appeal concerning its own interpretative competence!

I say in all seriousness and in all modesty that these are problems which will lead outsiders to distrust us so long as we remain unprepared to resolve and settle them. At the same time they are problems which can only be settled within the framework of a *free atmosphere* which is as open as possible and devoid of fear. Is it unfair of a theologian to express this question openly and to risk this act of honesty internally and externally?

Let these allusions suffice, my Lord Bishop, to make clear to you yet again that my 'inquiry' of some years ago, which conspicuously achieved so much publicity, was both urgently necessary and called for by the matter in hand.

Questions, Doubts and Denial

With reference to the matter of infallibility the German bishops have declared that I have not simply asked about the meaning and basis of the definition. Rather I am alleged to have 'jeopardised this proposition itself and hence to have doubted it'. I believe that this distinction fails to get to grips with the intricacies of the problem. Under the impulse of questions posed by many people, I as a theologian expressly inquired into the reasons for this definition. The effect of this 'inquiry' has perhaps been that the infallibility definition has seemed to many to be without proper foundation in terms of the present state of theological research. This doubt was not arbitrarily broached by myself as if I were pitting my own against the Church's interpretation of the faith. On the contrary, this doubt springs from the exegenies inherent in argument and counter-argument, a factor which is quite independent of my person.

Thus I made a formal 'inquiry' and did not issue any outright denial, and I believe that I did so under the prompting of an ecclesial disposition. For I never thought of coming forward with the pretension of one who would declare a universally defined proposition void. I have simply practised the sometimes troublesome, because risky, business of theology. I believe, my Lord Bishop, that anyone who puts his trust in the power of faith certainly also possesses the power of standing up to all the questions which human reason addresses to faith. The opposite also holds true, so that anyone who is ready and able to face up to any questions without prematurely forbidding them thereby affords proof of the unbroken power of his own faith.

In virtue of this basic attitude I place myself without reservation behind the above-mentioned statement of German theologians: 'In order to discharge its responsibility as a branch of academic study, theology must be able to make unqualified use of the freedom to take into its service all methods suitable for research into and exposition of the faith. There can never be too much freedom to follow where the subject matter leads and to employ the methods which it dictates, nor can the use of this freedom ever be tantamount to arbitrariness. It can therefore never be the responsibility of the episcopal teaching office to direct or recommend theology to use certain methods and to forbid it to use others, but—in the event of its being necessary—to point out in its official capacity when an interpretation attained by this or that method cannot be regarded as a legitimate exposition of the authentic faith attested in the faith of the Church and proclaimed by pope and bishops. With the declaration of 1969 on "The Freedom of Theologians and of Theology", which was signed by 1,360 theologians, we emphasise that "This freedom [means] for us theologians the grave responsibility of not endangering the genuine unity and the true peace of the Church and all its members". At the same time we must affirm with the same declaration that we "wish to discharge our duty of seeking and saying the truth without obstruction by administrative measures and sanctions. We expect our freedom to be respected when we voice or publish our substantiated theological convictions in good conscience and in accordance with our best knowledge".'

Translated by John Stephenson

Contributors

JAMES BARR is now Regius Professor of Hebrew in the University of Oxford. He was born in Glasgow in 1924 and was ordained to ministry of the Church of Scotland in 1951. He has been professor of Old Testament, Edinburgh, 1955-61; of Old Testament, Princeton Theological Seminary, New Jersey, 1961-5; of Semitic Languages and Literatures, Manchester University, England, 1965-76; Oriel Professor of the Interpretation of Holy Scripture, Oxford, 1976-8. He has held main visiting professorships in: Hebrew University, Jerusalem, 1973; University of Chicago, 1975; Strasbourg, 1975-6. His books include *The Semantics of Biblical Language* (1961); *Biblical Words for Time* (2nd edition with new chapter added, 1969); *Old and New in Interpretation* (1966); *The Bible in the Modern World* (1973).

FERNANDO BELO was born in 1933, qualified as a civil engineer in 1956 and became a priest in 1961, all these in Lisbon, where he was for four years military and high school chaplain and parish priest of a working-class suburb. He gained a degree in theology at Louvain in 1967 and a further degree in Paris in 1968. Married at the time, with two children, he worked six hours a day as a computer operator in a Paris physics laboratory and attended the seminars of Barthes, Greimas, Kristeva and seminars on Althusserian sociology while writing his *Lecture matérialiste de l'évangile de Marc*. He returned to Portugal after the outbreak of the movement of 25 April 1974 and worked in television making documentaries on the peasants. Since 1975 he has taught linguistic philosophy in the Faculty of Letters in Lisbon. He is now divorced.

JOSEF BLANK was born in Ludwigshafen, Federal Republic of Germany, in 1926 and ordained in 1951. He studied at Tübingen, Munich and Würzburg and since 1969 has been professor for New Testament exegesis and biblical theology at Saarbrücken. Among his published works are *Krisis* (1964); *Paulus und Jesus* (1968); *Schriftauslegung in Theorie und Praxis* (1969); *Jesus von Nazareth* (1972); *Das Evangelium nach Johannes* (1977).

ALLAN AUBREY BOESAK was born in 1946, and studied in Cape Town, New York, Amsterdam and Kampen, gaining his doctorate in theology from the Theologische Hogeschool, Kampen, Netherlands. He is at present chaplain to students at the University of Western Cape. He is also national chairman of the Association for Christian Students of South Africa. He has written *Farewell to Innocence* A Social-ethical Study of Black Theology and Black Power (1977) (British title: *Black Theology, Black Power*); and *Die Vinger von God* Sermons on faith and politics (1979) (English and German texts in preparation).

BERNADETTE BROOTEN was born in 1951 and has studied at the University of Portland (Oregon), the University of Tübingen, Harvard University and the Hebrew University of Jerusalem. In 1978/79 she held the position of Research/Resource Associate in Women's Studies at Harvard Divinity School, and is presently writing a doctoral dissertation for Harvard University entitled, 'Women as Leaders in Paul and in the Ancient Synagogue'. At the moment she is Visiting Assistant Professor at the School of Theology at Claremont and the Claremont Graduate School. She is a member of several scholarly societies, a Kent Fellow and a regular contributor to the homiletical publication, *Good News*. She has also contributed to L. and A. Swidler, *Women Priests. A Catholic Commentary on the Vatican Declaration* (1977), and is about to publish 'The Gospel in Conflict. Paul's Opponents in Galatians': *The Bible Today*.

ALEXANDRE GANOCZY was born in Budapest in 1928. He studied at the Pazmany University there, at the Institut Catholique in Paris and at the Gregorian University in Rome. He is a doctor of theology and philosophy and is professor of systematic theology at the University of Würzburg. He has published a number of articles and books, including *Le Jeune Calvin* (1966); *Ecclesia ministrans* (1968); *Sprechen von Gott in heutiger Gesellschaft* (1974); *Der schöpferische Mensch und die Schöpfung Gottes* (1976); *Einführung in die katholische Sakramentenlehre* (1979).

CHRISTIAN HARTLICH, a Protestant, was born in 1907 and studied classical philology, philosophy and theology at Tübingen, Berlin and Leipzig, where he took his degree in 1939. A member of the synod of the Confessing Church in Saxony, he was a teacher at grammar schools in Dresden and Tübingen. He lectured on the pedagogy of religious instruction at the Protestant faculty of theology at Tübingen university and was subsequently rector of the newly founded Protestant boarding-school at Pforte in Westphalia. He is now retired. His works include *Einführung in das Problem der Entmythologisierung*, written jointly with W. Sachs, which appeared in *Für Arbeit und Besinnung* no. 4 (1950) and was partially reprinted in *Kerygma und Mythos* II (1952), and *Der Ursprung des Mythosbegriffes in der modernen Bibelwissenschaft*, again written jointly with W. Sachs, published in 1952.

RENÉ KIEFFER was born in Aumetz, France in 1930 and brought up in Luxembourg. He studied philosophy and languages in Luxembourg, Paris, Fribourg and Munich, gaining his doctorate in 1954. From 1955-62 he studied philosophy and theology at Le Saulchoir, and then went on to do exegetical studies at the Ecole Biblique in Jerusalem. He has been resident in Sweden since 1965, and since 1972 has been Dean of New Testament Studies at the State University of Lund. His publications include: *Au delà recensions? L'évolution de la tradition textuelle dans Jean VI, 52-71* (doctoral thesis) (1968); *Essais de méthodologie néo-testamentaire* (1972); *Le primat de l'amour. Commentaire épistémologique de 1 Corinthiens 13* (1975); *Nytestamentlig teologi* (1977). He has also written articles and reviews in English, French, German and Swedish New Testament theological journals.

PINCHAS LAPIDE, who was born in Vienna in 1922, has spent many years as a diplomat in the service of the Israeli Foreign Ministry. He has held teaching appointments in Jerusalem and in Germany, including a period as Visiting New Testament Professor at Göttingen. Among his publications are a number of works dealing with the Jewish understanding of Jesus, and relations between Jews and Christians.

CARLOS MESTERS was born in Holland in 1931, went to Brazil as a seminarian in 1949, entered the Carmelite Order and was ordained in 1957. He graduated with honours in theology from the University of St Thomas in Rome, spent two years at the Ecole Biblique in Jerusalem, gaining a licentiate in Sacred Scripture from the Pontifical Biblical Commission. He has published several books on biblical subjects, and now directs the Centre of Biblical Studies for Pastoral Care of the People.

DOMINIQUE STEIN was born in Paris in 1931. After having studied in the Faculty of Medicine in Paris and specialised in neuro-psychiatry she became a psycho-analyst. She was an active member of the Société Psychanalytique de Paris from 1962-79. She has published numerous clinical and theoretical psycho-analytical articles, as well as poems, in *L'Inconscient, Revue Française de Psychanalyse, Etudes Freudiennes*. She has also written a study of St Theresa of Lisieux in *La Vie spirituelle* (1972), on the status of women in the letters of St Paul in *Lumiere et Vie* (1978) and a review of Francoise Dolto's book *L'Evangile au risque de la psychanalyse in Jésus* (1979).

Studies Review

Religious

A publication like *Religious Studies Review* has been needed for a long time in our field. We now have in the *Review* a thoroughly responsible organ dedicated to reviewing the critical books in the field of religion and related disciplines—it is high time and many of us are very, very grateful for it.
> *Sally McFague, Dean, Vanderbilt Divinity School*

Religious Studies Review is a sign of maturity in the discipline, and a guide to the wealth of resources now available. Its scholarly approach and critical stance provide perspective in an area tempted to live beyond its means.
> *Joseph C. McLelland, Dean, Faculty of Religious Studies*
> *McGill University*

Religious Studies Review dramatically documents the extent to which American scholarship in religion has come of age after having achieved corporate self-consciousness only so recently. In the Review Essays each issue of *RSR* bristles with material relevant for anyone concerned with religious studies in its wider scope, while the Notes on Recent Publications, organized according to topic areas, provide prompt contact with the stream of books and monographs that continue to emerge from presses throughout the world. The listing of recently completed Dissertations in Religion is an added bonus.
> *Robert A. Kraft, Chairperson, Department of Religious Studies*
> *University of Pennsylvania*

I have become an enthusiastic, regular reader of *Religious Studies Review*. It keeps me abreast of scholarly developments and current literature in my own and in other fields in a helpful, readable way.
> *Robert T. Handy, Academic Dean and Professor of Church History*
> *Union Seminary, New York, and Adjunct Professor of Religion*
> *Columbia University*

Annual Subscription Rates

Individuals belonging to member societies of the CSR: $10.00
Others (including institutions): $15.00

Make checks payable to **Council on the Study of Religion**, and mail to Council on the Study of Religion, Wilfrid Laurier University, Waterloo, Ontario   N2L 3C5

Oxford University Press

Living the Faith
A Call to the Church
Edited by Kathleen Jones

In this collection of essays a group of Anglican clergy and laity explores some of the challenges facing the Church today in a time of violent social and economic change, and the need for a liberal response to them. As members of the Open Synod Group they believe that a truly Christian approach to society is characterised by openness: by a willingness to learn from new developments, to receive fresh insights, and to examine new ideas. £5·95 paper covers £2·50

Edmund Campion
Scholar, Priest, Hero, and Martyr
Evelyn Waugh

'It is a joy to have available in paperback Evelyn Waugh's little masterpiece: *Edmund Campion*. We have not only a well authenticated picture of a man of exceptional goodness, courage, and charm, but one of the period in which he lived.' *Catholic Herald.* *Oxford Paperbacks* £2·50

All for Christ
Some Twentieth-Century Martyrs
Diana Dewar

It is not widely known that already in the twentieth century there have probably been more Christian martyrs than in all previous centuries combined. In this book the author tells the stories of eleven of those who died as martyrs in the last forty years, all from different countries and cultures. Illustrated £4·95. *Oxford Paperbacks* £1·95

Persecution in the Early Church
Herbert Workman

Persecution of the Church is now more widespread than it has ever been. No book portrays more graphically for the general reader the sufferings of the martyrs of the first Christian centuries than *Persecution in the Early Church* which was originally published in 1906 and has since achieved the status of a classic. *Oxford Paperbacks* £1·95